HUMAN MEMORY
The Processing of Information

HUMAN MEMORY
The Processing of Information

GEOFFREY R. LOFTUS
ELIZABETH F. LOFTUS
University of Washington

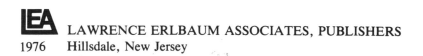

LAWRENCE ERLBAUM ASSOCIATES, PUBLISHERS
1976   Hillsdale, New Jersey

DISTRIBUTED BY THE HALSTED PRESS DIVISION OF

JOHN WILEY & SONS

New York   Toronto   London   Sydney

Lawrence Erlbaum Associates, Inc., Publishers
62 Maria Drive
Hillsdale, New Jersey 07642

Distributed solely by Halsted Press Division
John Wiley & Sons, Inc., New York

Library of Congress Cataloging in Publication Data

Loftus, Geoffrey R
  Human memory.

  Bibliography: p.
  Includes indexes.
  1. Memory. 2. Human information processing.
I. Loftus, Elizabeth F., 1944–   joint author.
II. Title. [DNLM: 1. Memory. BF371 L829h]
BF371.L64   153.1'2   75-20266
ISBN 0-470-54336-1
ISBN 0-470-54337-X pbk.

Printed in the United States of America

77-4438

This book is dedicated to
the memory of
EFL's Father,
Dr. Sydney A. Fishman
1913–1975

Contents

Preface

Over the past 20 years, the study of human memory has become an increasingly popular topic of study for psychologists, and since the late 1960s a new framework for studying memory has begun to take shape. It is the purpose of this book to present a broad overview of this framework, including descriptions of (1) the major theoretical components of the framework and (2) the critical research findings that justify the establishment of these components and illuminate the mechanisms by which they operate. The book is not meant to constitute an exhaustive review of the enormous research literature that has accrued over the years. We deliberately avoid wading into masses of detail on any given topic area, and we deliberately sidestep a number of current theoretical controversies. Instead, we have planned this book to be a guide and an introduction for the student or interested layman with little or no background in the area of memory as a field of psychological inquiry. We seek primarily to describe the forest, and we provide some direction to a number of other excellent texts that recount the details of the trees.

As suggested by our title, the theoretical framework with which this book is concerned views the *processing of information* as the principal mental task engaged in by human beings. A person is seen as constantly taking in information from the environment and then storing, manipulating, and recoding portions of this information in a succession of memory stages. The key tasks involved in the scientific investigation of memory are seen as (1) identification of the memory stages themselves and (2) the investigation of what types of information processing characterize each stage.

The organization of the book loosely reflects the way memory is conceived to be organized within this information-processing framework. Following a short introductory chapter, Chapters 2–4 describe the three major stages, or repositories of memorial information: sensory store (which contains a brief, but complete, representation of the original sensory input); short-term store (roughly identifiable with "consciousness"); and long-term store (which contains the vast amount of information that is permanently or semipermanently available to an individual). Chapters 5 – 7 then deal with specific types of memory situations. Chapter 5 describes the process by which we recognize information as being information we have encountered before; Chapter 6 explores the means by which we assimilate rich, naturalistic, meaningful information such as prose; and Chapter 7 describes how well-learned semantic information is represented in and retrieved from memory. Finally, Chapter 8 delves into four areas of technology to which theory and research from the information-processing framework may be applied. Chapter 8 also serves as a summary of the preceding seven chapters.

Friends and colleagues have contributed to this book in various ways. The initial drafts of several of the chapters benefited greatly from the critical comments of Buz Hunt, Colin MacLeod, and Tom Nelson. Two anonymous reviewers painstakingly read various versions of the first draft, and the excellent critiques that resulted have figured heavily in the final manuscript. Ms. Margo Denke donated some of the best years of her life to what seemed like an endless stream of typing, editing, organizing, obtaining reproduction permissions, and the seven million or so other tasks involved in the physical preparation of the manuscript. Finally, we express our hearty appreciation to all the people at Lawrence Erlbaum Associates who, from start to finish, have been doing their best to make the whole publishing business a little less of a mystery to us.

GEOFFREY R. LOFTUS
ELIZABETH F. LOFTUS
Seattle, Washington

1
Introduction

According to *Guinness' Book of Records*, the longest moustache ever to flourish under the nose of man was grown in India and spanned a prodigious 102 inches.

Unless you are an avid afficionado of trivia, the preceding sentence has probably told you things you didn't know before. In particular, it has told you the length and location of the world's longest moustache. It has also told you that these facts are recorded in *Guinness' Book of Records*. Let's zero in for a minute on one of these facts: the moustache length of 102 inches. Close your eyes for a few seconds and then try to recall this number. Chances are you are able to do it. Chances are that you could also, if asked, recall it in 10 minutes. If you spend enough time right now memorizing the number, you could probably also remember it next month.

A human being presented with some new fact is often able to reproduce the fact some period of time later. During that period of time, the fact, or some representation of it, must have been stored somewhere within the individual. Therefore, humans possess memory.

What is memory? Implicitly, we have defined memory above as some kind of repository in which facts (information) may be retained over some period of time. If this simple definition is accepted, however, memory is possessed not only by humans but by a great number of other things as well. Trees, for example, have memory, for a tree retains information about its own age by adding a new layer or ring to itself every year. A tree also occasionally stores information about events that happen to it in its lifetime. For instance, suppose lightning strikes it one night, leaving a black disfiguring gash in its trunk. The gash remains forever as part of the tree, thereby providing a "memory" of the event.

We feel in our hearts, however, that the memory possessed by a human is somehow more sophisticated than the memory possessed by a tree and, with a little thought, we can enumerate some differences between tree memories and human memories. First, a tree is severely limited in terms of the type of information it can put into its memory. A tree stores information about its own age in its "memory" (and occasionally information about lightning strikes), but it cannot store information about the world's longest moustache. (Some trees store information about romances—for example, GL loves BF—but this sort of information is carved into the tree by humans and not put there by the tree itself.) Humans, in contrast, are capable of putting any arbitrary information in their memories; you saw evidence of this a few minutes ago when you stored information about the world's longest moustache.

A second difference between trees and humans is that a tree does not have the ability to retrieve information from its memory and present the retrieved information to the outside world on request. No matter how many different ways I ask a tree how old it is, it won't tell me. I have to cut it down, count the rings, and find out for myself. In contrast, if I request information residing in the memory of a human, he[1] has the ability to retrieve that information and communicate it to me. The specific means by which the request for information is made and the specific manner in which the information is communicated may differ in different situations. If, for example, I want to know your name, I simply ask you and you communicate it to me vocally. However, if I'm in a Paris restaurant and want information about where the bathroom is from a waiter who speaks no English, my request for this information and his communication of it to me may take the form of elaborate gestures. Other idiosyncratic means of requesting information may be necessary when, for example, a mother is confronted with an infant too young to speak. In each of these cases, however, the person from whom the information is being requested has the capability of retrieving it and communicating it in one way or another.

In short, a human has not only a memory but an elaborate memory *system*. We have just noted a few things about this system: that it has the capability of putting new information into a memory and of retrieving information already in memory. An additional characteristic of the system not noted above is that some information in memory seems to become less available over time. In 1972, I lived in New York and had a New York telephone number. In 1972, that number was available to my memory system. Now it's not. In common parlance, things get forgotten.

The subject matter of this book is a detailed specification of the human memory system. Basically, we shall try to describe how the system puts

---

[1] There are many anonymous human beings to whom this book refers only by pronouns. This group of individuals consists of both men and women. In the interest of stylistic simplicity, however, only the masculine pronouns will be used. When used in this book, therefore, the pronoun, "he" may refer either to "he" or to "she" or to "he or she". Likewise, the pronoun, "him" may refer either to "him" or to "her" or to "him or her." Likewise, the pronoun, "his" may refer either to "his" or to "hers" or to "his or hers."

information into memory, how it retrieves information from memory, and what happens to information resident in memory.

THE INFORMATION-PROCESSING APPROACH

We have been discussing memory in terms of *information*, which has been loosely viewed as some kind of substance that is put into memory, retrieved from memory, lost from memory, etc. This information-oriented way of talking about memory is relatively recent, having been used by theorists only since the 1950s. Two major events were in large part responsible for stimulating this approach: the development of information theory and the development of computers. Before we proceed, we shall briefly describe the relevance of these two events to the information-processing approach to memory.

Information theory.   We all have an intuitive view of what information is. When I tell you something you didn't know before, you've acquired information. For example, you acquired information when you read about the length of the world's longest moustache. However, suppose I tell you that the world's southernmost continent is Antarctica. Have I told you something? Yes. Have you acquired information? No, because I didn't tell you anything you didn't already know.

In 1949, Shannon and Weaver took this intuitive notion of information and quantified it; that is, they showed how information could be made measureable. To quantify information, the first thing needed was a unit of measurement. To measure volume, we have cubic centimeters; to measure distance, we have inches. To measure information, we have *bits*. A bit is defined as: the amount of information that distinguishes between two equally likely alternatives. I've just flipped a coin. In telling you that the outcome of the flip was tails I've conveyed to you 1 bit of information, since prior to my telling you the outcome there were, as far as you were concerned, two equally likely outcomes to the flip.

More generally, suppose that some situation has N equally likely outcomes. (For example, if I roll a die, $N = 6$; if I tell you I'm thinking of a digit, $N = 10$; if I tell you I'm thinking of a letter of the alphabet, $N = 26$.) The amount of information you acquire when appraised of the outcome of the situation can be expressed by the following equation:

$$I = \log_2 N,$$

where I is a measure of the amount of information. This equation may be read: "the amount of information is equal to the base-two logarithm of the number of possible alternatives. Table 1.1 shows the amount of information in various stimuli according to this equation.

Readers not familiar with logarithms need not worry. For the purposes of this book, it is not important to know exactly *how* to quantify information.

TABLE 1.1

The Amount of Information in Various Types of Stimuli

Stimulus	N = number of alternatives	$I = \log_2 N$
Coin flip	2	1.00
Digit	10	3.32
Letter of the alphabet	26	4.70
U. S. state	50	5.65
Playing card	52	5.75
Squares of a checkerboard	64	8.00

What is important is the idea that the information contained in various stimuli *can* be quantified and we can therefore see that some stimuli (for example, letters) contain more information than other stimuli (for example, digits).

Recoding of information. Let us go back to our coin flip. Suppose I flip a coin and the outcome is tails. As we have seen, the outcome represents 1 bit of information; however, this 1 bit may take on a variety of physical representations. The coin itself lying on my wrist is one physical representation. If I say "tails," that is another representation of the same information.

Changing the form of the same information from one representation to another is called *recoding*. Consider a somewhat more complex array of information: the configuration of a checkerboard. Figure 1.1a shows one representation of the same information; Figure 1.1b shows quite a different representation of the same information. To get Figure 1.1b, I took the information in Figure 1.1a and recoded it. Figure 1.1c shows yet another representation that is a recoding of the information in Figure 1.1b. Notice an interesting thing: the recoding from Figure 1.1a to Figure 1.1b has preserved all of the original information. Therefore, Figure 1.1b could, if desired, be used to produce Figure 1.1a as well as vice versa. In the recoding from Figure 1.1b to Figure 1.1c, however, a good deal of the original information—namely, the position of the checkers—has been lost, and Figure 1.1c could not be used to reconstruct Figure 1.1b or Figure 1.1a. When information is recoded, therefore, it is possible for some of the original information to be lost.

In subsequent chapters, when we discuss the memory system, we shall see that the system includes components or *stages* of memory and that information passes from stage to stage. In passing from stage to stage, information is recoded, and in the process of being recoded, a good deal of information gets lost.

(a)

Square	Occupant	Square	Occupant	Square	Occupant	Square	Occupant
1	White	17	None	33	None	49	None
3	White	19	None	35	Black	51	Black
5	White	21	White	37	White	53	White
7	White	23	None	39	Black	55	None
10	None	26	None	42	None	58	Black
12	None	28	Black	44	White	60	None
14	Black	30	Black	46	None	62	Black
16	None	32	None	48	White	64	None

(b)

Nine white checkers

Eight black checkers

(c)

FIGURE 1.1 Recoding of information. Each panel provides information about the configuration of checkers on a checkerboard: (a) representation by a picture; (b) representation by a list; (c) representation in terms of numbers of black and white checkers.

Computers.   An important tool for any scientific theory is a *model* or physical analog of that about which one is attempting to theorize. For the atomic theory of Niels Bohr, the model is a tiny solar system with planets (electrons) spinning in their orbits about the sun (nucleus). For stimulus–response psychologists, the model is a telephone switchboard with calls coming in from the environment (stimuli) being routed via switchboard connections to the appropriate telephone (responses). For psychologists working within an information-processing framework, a computer provides an apt analogy of what is happening inside a person's head. The old view of a computer as a "giant brain" is taken seriously, except that it is somewhat reversed—a human brain is seen as a "midget computer." Both computers and people are information-processing systems, and Figure 1.2 shows a schematic view of the analogy. Both computers and humans take in information from the environment. Computers do this using card readers, tape drives, etc., whereas humans do it using their sense organs. Inside a computer, the information from

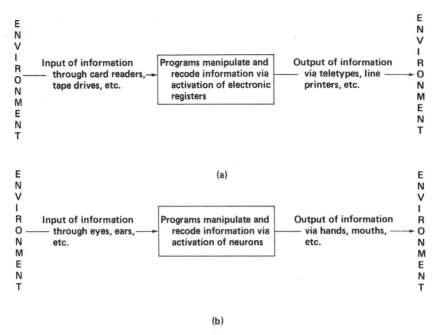

FIGURE 1.2   Similarity of information processing in computers and in humans: (a) computers; (b) people.

the environment is manipulated, recoded, and combined with other information already there. This is done via activation of electronic registers. Inside a person, information is manipulated, recoded, and combined with other information already there. This is done via activation of neurons. Finally, a computer outputs information to the environment via output devices, such as teletypes and line printers. Likewise, humans output information to the environment via such output devices as mouths and hands.

To extend the analogy, a distinction can be made at this point between computer hardware and computer software. Computer *hardware* is that which is built into the computer at the time it is made—the nuts and bolts, the metal frame, the transistors, resistors, and circuitry. Analogously, the "hardware" of a person consists of a body, of bones, of a complex system of neural circuitry, and so on. In contrast, computer *software* consists of *programs*, which cause the computer to manipulate information in various ways. A program is simply a series of instructions, written in a language the computer is built to understand, that tells the computer precisely what to do with the information presented to it. Programs are not built into the computer; instead they must be put in or "learned" by the computer. Furthermore, any arbitrary program can be put into any arbitrary computer.

Humans can also be thought of as possessing programs. For example, the capability of being able to add the numbers 321 + 714 was not built into me at birth. At some point, I had to learn how to add; that is, a program designed to carry out addition had to be put into me. On an even more complex level, my ability to ride a bicycle can be thought of as a program. Information about the state of the bicycle and myself on it comes in through sense organs. Inside my brain, the information is processed by my "bicycle riding program," resulting in the output of information to my arms and legs telling them what to do in order to keep the bicycle from falling over, to keep it going straight, and so on.

Using a computer analogy, therefore, human behavior is viewed as resulting from an interaction between information acquired from the environment and programs residing within the human that process and utilize this information. To extend and use the analogy as a basis for theorizing about human behavior, we note that computers (as do humans) exhibit, on the face of things, very complicated behavior. However, we know that the complicated behavior exhibited by computers is interpretable in terms of relatively simple, understandable computer programs. Now we speculate that the complicated behavior of humans may also be generated by relatively simple, understandable programs. The task of the information-processing oriented psychologist then becomes one of deducing (from experimental data) what these programs may look like.

A MODEL OF MEMORY

Up to now, we have been outlining what may be termed the philosophical basis for this book. In this section, we shall turn to something more concrete, and lay out a relatively simple, overall theory of how memory operates. In subsequent chapters, each component of the theory is examined in some detail.

The theory we shall discuss has been advanced in one form or another by a number of psychologists (for example Waugh & Norman, 1965; Glanzer, 1972) and was described in its most complete form by Richard Atkinson and Richard Shiffrin (Atkinson & Shiffrin, 1968, 1971). Atkinson and Shiffrin formulated the theory as a mathematical model; this meant that the theory's assumptions took the form of mathematical equations and that it made specific, quantitative predictions about the outcomes of various experiments. For our purposes, however, the mathematics may be bypassed and the theory discussed qualitatively.

Figure 1.3 represents a schematic (and somewhat oversimplified) view of the memory and information-processing system according to this theory. The boxes represent "stores" or repositories of information; the arrows represent the flow of information from place to place. To see how the system works, imagine that

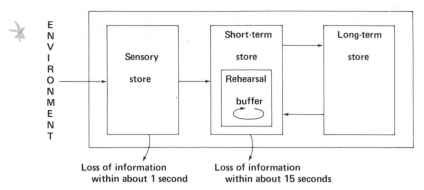

FIGURE 1.3   A schematic view of the two-store memory system.

you look up a telephone number, such as 325-5606. Let us trace the course of this information as it makes its way through the system.

The information first enters the system through one of your sense organs. In this case, the number is presented to you visually, so it enters through your eyes. The first store into which the information is placed is called *sensory store*. Sensory store can hold a large amount of information; in fact, it holds virtually all the information impinging on a particular sense organ. If you have looked up the number in the telephone directory, therefore, not only 325-5606 but all the other information on the page of the directory enters sensory store. However, information in sensory store decays away very quickly—in most cases, within a second or so. Therefore, unless information in sensory store is quickly transferred somewhere else, it will be lost.

Some of the information in the sensory store is indeed transferred into the next store, which is called *short-term store*. Short-term store (which may be introspectively equated with consciousness) has several major characteristics. First of all, it is of a limited capacity; it is large enough to hold one telephone number, but probably not large enough to hold two. Second, information in short-term store is, in general, lost within about 15 seconds; we have all had the experience of looking up a telephone number and walking across the room to dial it, only to discover that the number has been lost by the time we reached the telephone. However, information in short-term store may be placed into a special section of short-term store called a *rehearsal buffer*. Information in the rehearsal buffer does not decay away but may be maintained indefinitely via the process of *rehearsal*. Rehearsal means just what you think it means—that information is repeated over and over. So if you entered the number 325-5606 into your rehearsal buffer, you can maintain it by repeating to yourself "325-5606, 325-5606 . . ." for as long as you wish.

Which information gets entered into the rehearsal buffer? The theory assumes that people have the ability to enter whichever information they wish into the rehearsal buffer, allowing other information to decay away from short-term store. The choice of which information is to be entered and which is to be lost is presumably made in such a way that the person can carry out whatever task he is trying to do. So, for example, when you look up a person's number in the telephone directory, you may also find the person's address. If you wanted to call the person up, you would enter the number into your rehearsal buffer and allow the address to decay away. If, however, you intended to write the person a letter, it would be more prudent to enter the address into the rehearsal buffer and allow the number to decay away.

The final component of our system is long-term store. *Long-term store* is the virtually unlimited-capacity store of that information which we have more or less permanently available to us. For example, our own names, the multiplication table, our ability to speak a language, the days of the week, and so on are all stored in long-term store. How does all this information get into long-term store? It is assumed that while information resides in short-term store it can be copied or transferred into long-term store. The longer some particular information resides in short-term store, the more of that information can be transferred into long-term store. If you sit around repeating "325-5606" over and over to yourself, you are maintaining it in short-term store. Additionally, during this time, information about the number may be transferred to long-term store. In everyday language, you can memorize the number.

Suppose now you are called on to retrieve some information that has previously been presented to you—for example, suppose you have to dial the number you have looked up. You first check to see whether that information is in short-term store. If it is in short-term store, that's fine; you simply retrieve the information and use it. If the information is not in short-term store, you don't despair yet, for the information may have resided in short-term store long enough for it to be completely transferred to long-term store. Therefore, if the information is not in short-term store, you next search long-term store, and if the information is there it can be retrieved and used. (Retrieval and utilization of information from long-term store essentially consists of transferring information from long-term store to short-term store. This is represented by the arrow pointing left in Figure 1.3.) It is possible of course, that some but not all of the information has been transferred to long-term store. Thus, you may remember the exchange, 325, but not the rest. You may remember 325-560_, and remember that the last digit was even. You may have transferred the information corresponding to the digits themselves but not the information about their order, in which case you may retrieve the number 325-6506 and dial a wrong number.

This, then, is a very brief sketch of how the memory system is assumed to operate. The type of memory system we have described is often referred to as a *two-store system* in reference to its two major information stores, short-term store and long-term store. For each of the stores, we shall be concerned with four major questions:

1. How is information *represented* in the store?
2. How is information *lost* (forgotten) from the store?
3. How is information *retrieved* from the store?
4. How is information *transferred* from store to store; what types of recoding take place during transfer of information; and what, if any, information is lost when the information is recoded?

2

Sensory Store

At any given point in time, our five sense organs are being bombarded with a vast amount of information from the environment. At the present moment, for example, a complex array of *visual* information is entering my eyes in the form of light. This visual information represents the books on my shelves, the pictures on my walls, the rain splashing on my window, the words I am writing on a page, and a great many other things. At the same time, *auditory* information is impinging on my ears in the form of sound. The sound represents last night's baseball scores coming over the radio, the clicking of a typewriter in the next office, and the hum of conversations in rooms around me. Similarly, my sense of touch is receiving *tactile* information about my itchy wool sweater; my sense of smell is receving *olfactory* information about the perfume worn by the student who just passed my door and my sense of taste is receiving *gustatory* information about what's gone into the sandwich I'm eating.

Information impinging on the senses initially goes into what is called *sensory store*, which is the subject matter of this chapter. The term "sensory store" is actually a misnomer because there are several different sensory stores, one corresponding to each sensory modality. Visual information entering the eyes is initially placed into a visual sensory store, called *iconic store*. Auditory information entering the brain through the ears is initially placed into a sensory store corresponding to audition, called *echoic store*. Although there are other sensory stores corresponding to other modalities, psychologists have concentrated most of their research activity on iconic store and echoic store. This is because human behavior, for the most part, is based on information that is initially visual or auditory. Consequently, the discussion in this chapter is restricted to iconic and echoic store.

ICONIC STORE

As suggested in Chapter 1, iconic store is thought to be a complete but brief repository of all information that initially enters the brain through the eyes.[1] The first question we must deal with is: what leads us to believe that iconic store exists? What evidence supports the assertion that there is indeed a large-capacity visual store? A classic set of experiments performed by George Sperling in 1960 provides us with answers to these questions. Sperling's experiments laid the groundwork for a large amount of work dealing not only with iconic store but with sensory store in general, so we shall describe his experiments in some detail.

The information available in a brief visual presentation.   Sperling's discovery of iconic store began somewhat obliquely with the seemingly unrelated question: how much of a visual stimulus can a person see when that stimulus is presented for a very brief period of time? (By "very brief" we mean a period of time ranging from 10 to 200 milliseconds where a millisecond is 1/1000 of a second.) Sperling's major reason for investigating this question was that visual behavior in general is made up of a series of "brief visual presentations." Ask a friend to look around the room and watch his eyes as he does so. Notice that eyes do not describe a smooth, continuous motion as they move around. Instead, they are still for a brief period, quickly move to another position, are still for another brief period, move again, are still again, and so on. The periods during which the eyes are still are called *fixations*; the quick eye movements separating fixations are called *saccades* (saccade being French for "jump"). Visual information is taken in by the eyes during the fixation periods, whereas vision is essentially suppressed during saccades. Saccades occur at the rate of about three per second; each fixation therefore lasts for a period of about 300 milliseconds. We see then that the eye is constantly presenting the brain with a series of brief visual presentations in the form of fixations; therefore the question of how much a person can see during such a presentation becomes quite important.

Since the late 1800s numerous investigators (for example, McDougall, 1904; Whipple, 1914) have done numerous experiments dealing with this question. Arrays of items (for example, letter arrays such as those shown in Figure 2.1) have been briefly presented to a subject in a tachistoscope. (A tachistoscope is an optical device for presenting visual stimuli very briefly.

---

[1] To be precise, we should point out that visual information originally enters the eyes in the form of patterns of light. The patterns of light are then transformed at a very early stage into patterns of neural impulses, and it is the information contained in these neural impulse patterns that goes into iconic store. Visual information has therefore actually been recoded to some extent before it goes into iconic store. However, the nature of this early processing is not part of the scope of this book. We shall loosely assume therefore that the visual information goes directly from the environment into iconic store.

Many people have trouble pronouncing and remembering the word "tachisto-scope" so it's often just called a t-scope.) After he had viewed the array of letters, the subject in our typical experiment was simply asked to report back as many of the letters from the array as he could remember. Suppose we now plot the average number of letters reported by the subject as a function of the number of letters presented in the array. The results obtained by such a procedure are shown in Figure 2.2. If up to about four of five letters are presented, the subject is perfect; he is able to report them all back. The initial part of the curve in Figure 2.2 therefore rises linearly. However, if more than four or five letters are presented in the array, the subject is not able to report the additional letters but is still only able to report four or five. The curve in Figure 2.2 therefore flattens out after four or five letters. The conclusion drawn from studies such as this typical one is that the amount a person is able to see in a single brief visual presentation is apparently constrained to about four or five items. This finding has been replicated many times and the apparent limit of four or five letters has been given a name: it is called the *span of apprehension*.

As with many findings in psychology, however, this experimentally deter-mined span of apprehension was at odds with what subjects thought was happening. In particular, subjects had two introspective reports that conflicted with assumptions experimenters were making about the experimental situation. First, it was assumed that subjects had the capability of reporting *all* the letters they saw in the array, that is, that what was reported constituted a completely faithful index of what was seen. "Not so!" said the subjects. Consider an array of 12 letters. Although subjects could only report four or five of the 12 letters, it was not the case, they said, that they only saw the four or five letters they reported. Instead, the claim went, they saw virtually all of the letters but as they were writing down the first four or five, they forgot the last seven or eight.

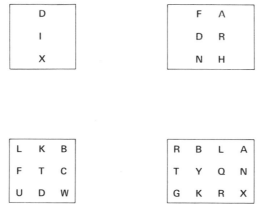

FIGURE 2.1   Arrays used in a typical experiment to measure the information available in a brief visual presentation.

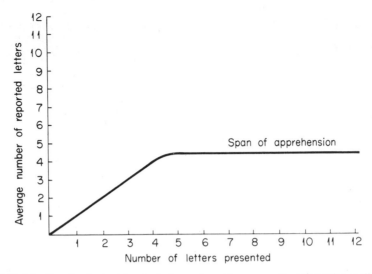

FIGURE 2.2   Results obtained in a typical experiment to measure the information available in a brief presentation.

According to this notion, then, the experimentally determined span of apprehension resulted not from a limit on how much could be seen but was instead caused by a limit on how much of what was seen could be retained.

The second assumption was that the amount of time the subjects had to perceive the array was exactly equal to the amount of time the array was presented. If an experimenter turned on the array of the t-scope, left it on for 50 milliseconds and then turned it off, it seemed only reasonable to expect that the subject had only those 50 milliseconds to perceive the array. Again, subjects disagreed. From their point of view, it did not appear as though the array was being abruptly turned off; it appeared to be gradually fading away over the course of a second or so. It therefore seemed that they were still seeing the 50 millisecond array for up to about 950 milliseconds after it had physically vanished.

Whole reports versus partial reports.   In the type of experiment just described, subjects were asked to report *all* the letters they could from the array; in other words, they were being asked to make a *whole report* of the letters in the array. According to the subjects, however, this was a very bad procedure, because as noted some letters were forgotten while others were being reported. To rectify this problem, Sperling devised a *partial report* procedure, depicted in Figure 2.3.

In a partial report procedure, as in a whole report procedure, the subject is initially presented with an array (say a 3 × 4 array) for 50 milliseconds. The twist is that the subject is not required to report all the letters in the array.

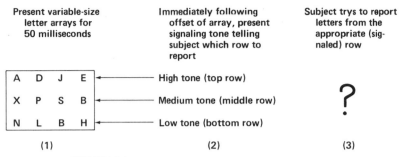

| Present variable-size letter arrays for 50 milliseconds | Immediately following offset of array, present signaling tone telling subject which row to report | Subject trys to report letters from the appropriate (sig-naled) row |

FIGURE 2.3   Sperling's (1960) partial report technique.

Instead, they are required to report only one four-letter row. The subject is told which row to report by means of a signal that occurs immediately after the array is turned off. The signal takes the form of a tone played to the subject through earphones. A high-frequency tone indicates that only the top row is to be reported; a medium-frequency tone indicates that only the middle row is to be reported; and a low-frequency tone indicates that only the bottom row is to be reported.

Using the number of letters per row that the subject was able to report using this procedure, Sperling was able to *estimate* the total number of letters the subject must have had available at the instant the array was turned off. Suppose, for example, that on the average, the subject was able to report three out of the four letters per row. Because the subject did not know beforehand which row he was going to have to report, this must mean that he had three letters available from each of the three rows. The total number of letters estimated to be available would therefore be three rows times three letters per row, or nine letters in all.

Sperling now performed the experiment described above, presenting arrays of letters for 50 milliseconds, varying the numbers of letters contained in the array, and seeing how much of the array subjects could report back. For each array size, however, the experiment was performed using both whole and partial report procedures. The results of this experiment are shown in Figure 2.4. For a whole report, the procedure is identical to that used in previous experiments, so the curve obtained in this condition is identical to the curve shown in Figure 2.2; it levels off at the four–five item span of apprehension. With the partial report procedure, however, the curve does not level off but continues to rise: the more letters presented in the array, the more letters are estimated to be available to the subject.

This result is very important, for it shows that the span of apprehension does not, as early experimenters assumed, accurately measure the amount of information that subjects are able to perceive. Instead, the result gives experimental support to the introspective feeling that during a brief visual presentation people are able to *see* more than they are ultimately able to *report*.

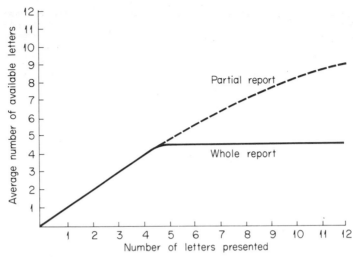

FIGURE 2.4   Results obtained in Sperling's (1960) first experiment. (After Sperling, 1960, Figure 3. Copyright 1960 by the American Psychological Association. Reproduced by permission.)

Fading images.   The second introspective report was that there was an image of a briefly presented visual stimulus that decayed away over the course of a second or so, outlasting the physical stimulus itself. Sperling's second experiment was aimed at investigating this notion.

Figure 2.5 shows the general setup of Sperling's second experiment, which differs somewhat from the one just described. First, whereas in the previous experiment array size has been varied, in the second experiment only one array size was used. For ease of discussion, let us assume that only a 12-letter array—three rows by four columns—was used. Second, in the second experiment, only a partial report procedure was used; on all trials, a signaling tone indicated to the subject which row to report. Finally, in the second experiment, the *delay time* between the offset of the array and the signaling tone was varied (remember that in the first experiment, the tone was always presented simultaneously with the offset of the array, that is, the delay time was always zero). Of primary interest in this experiment was the function relating estimated number of letters available to the subject to the delay time.

The results of past experiments tell us a few things about how the subject should behave in Sperling's second experiment. Consider first the zero-delay point (that is, the condition when the signaling tone is presented immediately at the offset of the array). With zero delay, a partial report procedure, and a 12-letter array, we can read off Figure 2.4 that about nine letters should be available to the subject. We have plotted this point on Figure 2.6. Next let us consider a very long delay interval, say 5 seconds. We know that if a *whole* report procedure were used, only about four or five letters would be available

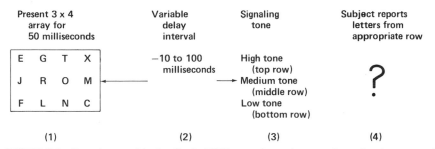

Present 3 x 4 array for 50 milliseconds	Variable delay interval	Signaling tone	Subject reports letters from appropriate row
E G T X J R O M F L N C	−10 to 100 milliseconds	High tone (top row) Medium tone (middle row) Low tone (bottom row)	?
(1)	(2)	(3)	(4)

FIGURE 2.5   Procedure used in Sperling's (1960) second experiment to determine decay rate of information from iconic store.

to the subject; this is just the old span of apprehension result. But since a partial report procedure is used, the subject will *report* only about one-third of four or five letters (because the subject is only reporting letters from one out of the three rows). Using our estimation procedure, however, we multiply the number of reported letters by 3 to obtain an *estimate* of four or five letters available to the subject. This point has also been plotted in Figure 2.6.

How will the function behave at delays other than these two? Consider two alternative possibilities. The first possibility is that the array of letters is available to the subject *only* during the 50 milliseconds that the array is physically present (as assumed by prior investigators). If this alternative is correct, then the function should be a step function; at delay times up to zero about nine letters should be available, whereas at delay times greater than zero the function should precipitously plummet to four or five letters, the span of

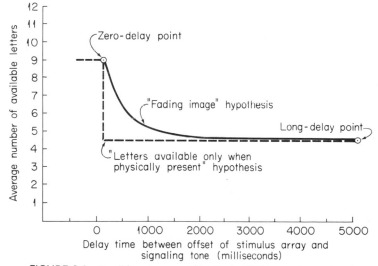

FIGURE 2.6   Possible outcomes of Sperling's (1960) second experiment.

apprehension. (Note that negative delay times simply mean that the signaling tone was presented *before* the offset of the array.) This possibility is depicted by the dashed line in Figure 2.6. The second possibility is that the subjects' introspections are correct and that, following the offset of the array there is a fading image of the array available to the subject, just as the array itself was available for the 50 milliseconds during which it was actually present. If this is the case then the number of letters estimated to be available to the subject should gradually decline from nine down to four or five. This alternative is depicted by the solid line in Figure 2.6.

The function actually obtained by Sperling is shown in Figure 2.7. As you can easily see, the subjects' introspections are once again vindicated; the results do support the notion of a gradually fading image. How long does it take for the image to decay away? In Sperling's experiment, the function levels off after a delay of about 1 second; we therefore infer that 1 second is about the amount of time it takes the image to decay away.

Taken together, these two experiments provide us with the picture of iconic store that we have presented at the outset of this chapter. The first experiment indicates that a large portion of visual information presented to a subject is perceived by him. The second experiment provides evidence that the information in a visual stimulus outlasts the physical presence of the stimulus. The fading image depicted in Figure 2.7 constitutes a memory—a very brief memory from which information decays away in a second or less, but nonetheless a memory. This memory is iconic store.

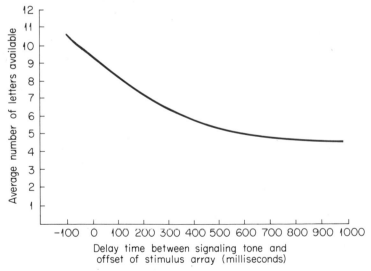

FIGURE 2.7   Results of Sperling's (1960) second experiment. (After Sperling, 1960, Figure 8. Copyright 1960 by the American Psychological Association. Reproduced by permission.)

ECHOIC STORE

We have just seen that Sperling's partial report technique has been highly successful in uncovering the existence of iconic store. How may this technique be modified to investigate an analogous "echoic store" for auditory information? Such a modification was devised in 1965 by Moray, Bates, and Barnett and was improved and extended in 1972 by Darwin, Turvey, and Crowder. As this latter experiment is somewhat more complete than the former, we shall discuss it.

The Darwin, Turvey, and Crowder experiment. The setup of the Darwin, Turvey, and Crowder (1972) experiment is shown in Figure 2.8. Subjects wore earphones; each earphone was connected to one channel of a stereo tape recorder. The experimental technique took advantage of a simple phenomenon that you can easily experience if you have a stereo and a pair of earphones. Put on the headphones, turn the stereo/mono switch to "mono" and listen to any record. Now turn the balance control all the way to the left and notice that the sound (which should only be coming out of the left earphone) appears to be coming from the left side of your head only. Analogously, if you now turn the balance control all the way to the right, the sound appears to be coming only from the right side of your head. With the balance right in the middle, the sound appears to be coming from the middle of your head. (You

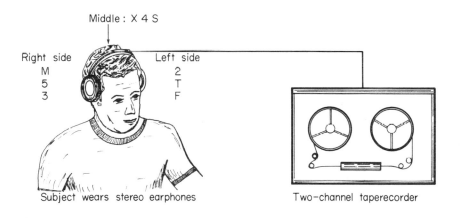

1. **Present nine letters:**   left   2 T F
                                middle   X 4 S
                                right   M 5 3
2. **Following last letters variable delay interval, 0—4000 milliseconds.**
3. **Signal bar presented on a screen. Bar is left of, in front of, or to right of subject.**
4. **Subject attempts to report channel signaled by bar.**

FIGURE 2.8   General setup of the Darwin *et al.* (1972) experiment.

can experience this without using the balance control if you listen with earphones, in stereo, to "A day in the life" by the Beatles. Paul McCartney's voice starts on the left side of your head, moves around your head to the right side, and then moves back to the left again. It's a very interesting experience even for someone not particularly interested in echoic store.)

In any event, Darwin *et al*. recorded nine items consisting of a mixture of letters and digits on a stereo tape in the following manner. Three items (for example, 2, T, F) were recorded on the left channel. Simultaneously, three different items (for example, M, 5, 3) were recorded on the right channel. Finally, superimposed in these two sets of items, three more items (for example, X, 4, S) were simultaneously recorded on both channels. Therefore, when the tape was played to a subject wearing stereo earphones, the subject simultaneously heard "2, T, F" coming from the left side of his head, "M, 5, 3" coming from the right side, and "X, 4, S" coming from the middle of his head. Now Darwin, Turvey, and Crowder were in a position to perform the auditory analog of Sperling's second experiment. They played the nine items to a subject and then, following a delay that ranged from 0 to 4 seconds, signaled the subject to report only the left, middle, or right channel. The signal used was a bar, flashed on a screen to the left, middle, or right of the subject. Darwin, Turvey, and Crowder, as did Sperling, also had a control condition in

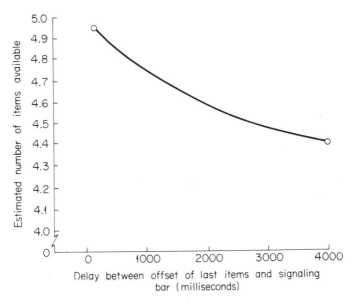

FIGURE 2.9   Results of the Darwin *et al*. (1972) experiment. (After Darwin *et al.*, 1972, Figure 2.)

which no signal was used, and the subjects tried to make a "whole report" of all the items in the array.

The results of this experiment, shown in Figure 2.9, look very much like Sperling's results, shown in Figure 2.7. With zero delay, five of the nine items are estimated to be available to the subject. With a delay of 4 seconds, the number of available items has dropped to 4.25, which is the span of apprehension—the number of items available using the whole report procedure. It may seem a little strange that with zero delay only five items are available. The reason for this low number is probably an unavoidable problem in the experiment: whereas the letters in Sperling's visual arrays can be shown all at once, the nine items in the Darwin *et al.* experiment have to be presented sequentially in groups of threes (where of course a group of three includes one item from each of the three channels). By the time the last group of three items is presented, therefore, the first group of three has had some time to decay away. The zero-delay point of five items is therefore probably an underestimate of the amount of information in echoic store at any given time.

From the results in Figure 2.9, we may infer the existence of an echoic store in exactly the same way we have inferred the existence of an iconic store from the results shown in Figure 2.7. The main difference between the two stores seems to be in terms of how long it takes information to decay from them. We have seen that it takes from 200 to 1000 milliseconds for information to decay from iconic store. The results of Figure 2.9 seem to indicate that decay of information from echoic store is not complete until about 4 seconds.

TYPE OF INFORMATION STORED IN SENSORY STORE

It is believed that information held in sensory store is raw, sensory information, as yet unanalyzed for meaning. To illustrate what is meant by this, suppose you are suddenly shown the visual pattern in Figure 2.10. By now, you probably know quite a bit about this visual pattern—that it is used to represent the letter "A," that there is a certain pronounciation associated with the pattern, that the pattern represents the first letter of the alphabet, and so on. However, at the instant you first perceived this pattern—that is, at the time the information about the pattern was residing in iconic store—this knowledge about what the pattern represented, what it *meant*, was not yet available to you. We shall see later that this information about meaning becomes available as a result of information being transferred from sensory store to short-term store.

What evidence supports the assertion that information in sensory story has not yet been analyzed for meaning? A third experiment performed in the series by Sperling (1960) provides us with such evidence. In this experiment,

FIGURE 2.10   A visual pattern.

Sperling used arrays such as the one shown in Figure 2.11. These arrays contained not just letters, but a mixture of letters and digits. Sperling now used the usual control condition of whole report, plus two types of partial report conditions. The first partial report condition was just like that used in prior experiments; the subject was simply instructed (with a high or low tone) to report either the top row or the bottom row. As expected, subjects in this condition showed a marked advantage over the whole report condition in terms of number of available symbols (letters and digits). In the second partial report condition, a high tone indicated that only the digits were to be reported, whereas a low tone indicated that only the letters were to be reported. Suppose now there is information in iconic store about whether a particular symbol is a letter or a digit (that is, information about the *meaning* of the symbol). In this case, the partial report advantage should still appear. For example, a subject signaled to report only letters could simply scan through iconic store picking out the letters and ignoring the digits much in the same way as he can go through picking out, say, only the top row symbols and ignoring the bottom row symbols. However, the partial report advantage did not materialize in the letter–digit condition. Using a partial report based on letters versus digits, the number of symbols estimated to be available to the subject was only four or five letters, which was no better than the number of symbols estimated in the whole report procedure. The conclusion that must be drawn from this result is that when an array of the sort shown in Figure 2.11 is in iconic store, the eight symbols are, as far as the subject is concerned, simply visual patterns. The subject does not yet have the ability to distinguish among the patterns in terms of what the patterns represent, whether they are letters or digits.

TRANSFER OF INFORMATION FROM SENSORY STORE TO SHORT-TERM STORE

We have just noted that information cannot really be used while it is still in sensory store. If, for example, I present you with the visual pattern, ''stop,'' you cannot base any behavior on the presentation of this pattern until you have decided what it means. Before information can be of any real value, therefore,

| 2 | G | 9 | T |
| F | 8 | 5 | R |

FIGURE 2.11   Types of arrays used in Sperling's (1960) third experiment.

it must be transferred out of sensory store and into some other store where meaning becomes attached to it. In this section we shall examine some characteristics of this transfer process.

Pattern recognition.   Pattern recognition is the term used to describe the process of transferring information from sensory store to short-term store. As we shall see, the term "pattern recognition" is used to describe this transfer process because the process essentially consists of "recognizing" a raw, physical pattern in sensory store as representing something meaningful. Pattern recognition is extremely complex and, at this point, not terribly well understood. In this book, pattern recognition is discussed only briefly. For more complete discussions of pattern recognition, the reader is directed to Neisser (1967) and to Lindsay and Norman (1972).

In order to discuss pattern recognition, let us elaborate on the distinction, made earlier, between a *symbol* (say a visually presented symbol) and a *concept*, which that symbol is used to represent. Figure 2.12 illustrates this distinction. On the left side of Figure 2.12 are shown various visual symbols. On the right side are described, to some extent, the concepts those symbols are used to represent. The first symbol, for example, is the pattern "A." As noted previously, the concept represented by the physical pattern "A" constitutes a complex array of information, including pronunciation rules, first letter of the alphabet, first letter of the word "apple," vowel, last letter of the word "pizza," and so on. The process of recognizing a pattern, then, consists of deciding which of all possible concepts a particular pattern corresponds to.

It is currently believed that this task is carried out via a *feature-detection* analysis. A particular pattern may be thought of as being made up of a collection of elementary features. The pattern "A" for example, can be thought of as having such features as two straight diagonal lines, one horizontal line, three acute angles, two oblique interior angles, etc. Figure 2.13 shows a

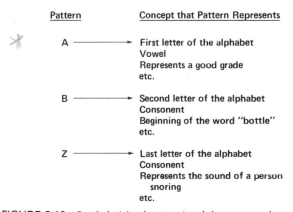

FIGURE 2.12   Symbols (visual patterns) and the concepts they represent.

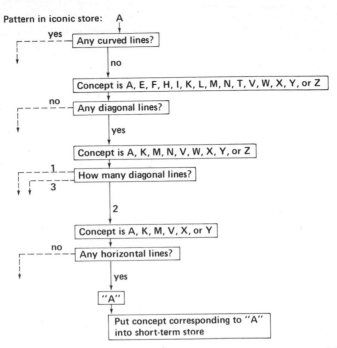

FIGURE 2.13   An example of how a hypothetical pattern-recognition program might recognize the physical pattern "A."

possible pattern recognition program that analyzes the raw patterns in sensory store and ultimately makes a decision as to what concept a particular pattern corresponds. In this example, the pattern "A" is presented and goes into iconic store from the environment. The pattern recognition program then begins to work on this input information by asking a series of questions about the physical features of the pattern. Based on the answers to these questions, the possible concepts to which the pattern might correspond are narrowed down until only one is left. The first question asked by our hypothetical program is: "does the pattern have a curved line?" Because the answer to this question is "No," the pattern must correspond to one of the all-straight-line letters, A, E, F, H, I, K, L, M, N, T, V, W, X, Y, or Z. The next question is, "does the pattern have at least one diagonal line?" The answer to this question further restricts the set of possible concepts to A, K, M, N, V, W, X, Y, or Z. This question–answer process continues until the range of possibilities has been narrowed to one. At this point, the pattern recognizer has decided that the pattern corresponds to an "A" and the information corresponding to the concept of an "A" is placed into short-term store.

Evidence for this kind of feature-testing model comes from a variety of sources and an extensive discussion of it is beyond the scope of this book.

However, to give a flavor for the relevant data, we shall briefly mention two types of evidence: behavioral evidence and physiological evidence.

Behavioral evidence for a feature-testing model has been gathered by Ulric Neisser and his colleagues, using what is termed a *visual-scanning task*. (Neisser, 1963, 1964, 1967; Neisser, Novak, & Lazar, 1963; see Egeth, 1967, for a review). Visual scanning is what you engage in when you enter a crowded bar or restaurant and search (scan) through the crowd to find a friend who was supposed to meet you there. Figure 2.14 shows how this task is implemented in the laboratory. On each of a series of trials, the subject is presented with a long array of letters. Somewhere in the array is a target letter (for example, the letter K) and it is the subject's job to scan through the array from top to bottom and to press a button immediately on finding the target. Of interest is how long it takes to search through all of the nontarget letters and to find the target.

Notice that the major process the subject undertakes is to *reject* nontargets as not being targets. If the feature-testing model is correct then it should be possible to systematically vary how long it takes the subject to reject nontargets by controlling how similar the nontargets are to the target. To see why this is so, compare the letter arrays depicted in Figure 2.14b and 2.14c with those depicted in Figures 2.14d and 2.14e. In Figures 2.14b and 2.14c the target is embedded in an array of similar nontargets, whereas in Figures 2.14d and 2.14c the target is embedded in a series of dissimilar nontargets. According to the feature-testing model, rejecting dissimilar nontargets should be a relatively

(a) Random nontargets: target is "K"	(b) Straight-line nontargets: target is "K"	(c) Round-line nontargets: target is "S"
CPLP	AXAA	GOOU
AYDC	AXLF	QOGG
DVFM	AFFH	UQGG
RNZD	LHXA	CQUQ
QSGA	LLFA	UOQC
DCIJ	AAKF	QCOU
QDQE	LALF	QUOS
BKFC	AALF	OQUQ
FYHO	AXHL	QCCU
IBVB	FXAX	OGCQ

(d) Straight-line nontargets: target is "S"	(e) Round-line nontargets: target is "K"
AXAA	GOOU
AXLF	QOGG
AFFH	UQGG
LHXA	CQUQ
LLFA	UOQC
AASF	QCOU
LALF	QOUK
AALF	OOUQ
AXHL	QCCU
FXAX	OGQC

FIGURE 2.14   Examples of arrays used in scanning experiments.

fast process because only a small number of features need be tested from any given candidate pattern. (In Figure 2.14b, the test would be "does the pattern have a curved line," whereas in Figure 2.14c, the test would be "does the pattern have a straight line.") With similar nontargets, however, the rejection process should be much slower because there is no one test that suffices to reject the candidate pattern; instead, the process is more like the one shown in Figure 2.13, where an extensive series of tests is needed. In short, if patterns are indeed recognized by a series of feature tests, then only a partial analysis of each nontarget is needed, and the more dissimilar the nontargets, the smaller the number of feature tests needed to accomplish the rejection.

If you ask a friend to find the target in the Figure 2.14 arrays, chances are that he will do the job faster for the dissimilar nontarget arrays than for the similar nontarget arrays—and in fact, this is exactly how subjects behaved in Neisser's experiments. Additionally, Neisser reports that subjects' introspections about the task provide further evidence: practiced subjects claim that during the scanning, most of the array "appears to be a blur," whereas the target "just pops out." Again, this is exactly what we should expect if only a partial, cursory analysis is being performed on nontargets; nontargets are never fully recognized (and may reasonably appear as a blur), whereas the target, of course, is fully recognized and thereby enters into consciousness (pops out).

In the physiology laboratory, an extensive series of experiments has been carried out by Hubel and Wiesel (1959, 1962) on response patterns of individual brain cells to various types of visual stimuli. Hubel and Wiesel's procedure involved anesthetizing a cat and then placing a tiny electrode into the portion of the cat's brain known as the visual cortex. When the electrode was indicating the activity of a single neuron, various simple visual stimuli were shown to the cat (which was still fully conscious). The findings were dramatic: certain cells responded only to very specific visual patterns. For instance, one cell responded only to a vertical line, another only to a horizontal line, and so forth. Such cells may therefore be viewed as elementary feature detectors and Hubel and Wiesel's confirmation of their existence provides fairly compelling support for a feature-testing model.

Figure 2.15 illustrates how the pattern-recognition process fits into the information-processing system discussed in Chapter 1. To briefly reiterate, the physical pattern "A" enters the eyes from the environment and is placed into iconic store. The pattern-recognition program then has the job of transferring this raw sensory information from sensory store into short-term store. In the process two things happen. First, the physical representation of the information is changed or recoded. (In Chapter 3 we shall see that the information is recoded into an acoustic form.) Second, the raw sensory information from the environment is supplemented by information already stored in long-term store.

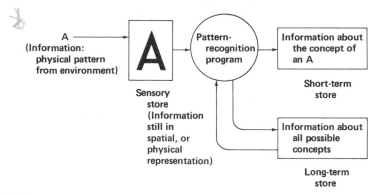

FIGURE 2.15   How a pattern-recognition program fits into the information-processing system.

Speed of pattern recognition.   In discussing our pattern recognition program, it has looked as though the program has a good deal to do. To completely recognize a pattern, the program must ask a long series of questions about the pattern, and it therefore seems that the process must be long and tedious. Exactly how long does pattern recognition take? This, of course, is a very important question, for the rate at which pattern recognition occurs places an initial limit on the speed with which we are able to interact with the environment. We shall describe two experiments dealing with this question that have been done by George Sperling.

Sperling (1963) has reported the first results germane to this question. The logic of this experiment is very simple and goes as follows: suppose we present a subject with a string of, say, five letters and, furthermore, suppose we vary the amount of time the string is presented. We then ask how many letters the subject is able to report back as a function of how long the string has been presented. We assume that in order that a letter from the string be reported, the letter must be pattern recognized. That is, information about the presence of that letter in the string must be transferred to short-term store. Now, suppose that one letter can be reported from a string that has been presented for 10 milliseconds, two letters can be reported from a string that has been presented for 20 milliseconds and so on. We then may assume that one letter can be pattern recognized every 10 milliseconds.

As you have no doubt figured out, this hypothetical experiment has a serious flaw; namely, it assumes that a subject can extract information from the letter string only when the string is physically present. However, we have seen that this assumption is false and that information can be extracted from the iconic image of the string for some time after the physical stimulus has disappeared. Fortunately, there is a way to correct this flaw. It turns out that if a briefly

1. Present a string of five letters. Presentation time varies from 5 to 200 milliseconds.

2. Follow string with a masking stimulus.

3. Masking stimulus erases letter string from iconic store.

FIGURE 2.16   Techniques used in Sperling's (1963) experiment.

presented visual stimulus is quickly followed by a second visual stimulus in the same spatial location (referred to as a *masking stimulus*) the masking stimulus erases the initial stimulus from iconic store, rendering it impossible for the subject to further extract information from the initial stimulus.

The design of Sperling's actual experiment is illustrated in Figure 2.16. The experiment went as follows: a string of letters was initially presented in a t-scope for a period of time ranging from 5 to 200 milliseconds and this string of letters was immediately followed by a masking stimulus. (For various reasons, the masking stimulus used by Sperling was a field of random bits and pieces of letters.) Notice the crucial role played by the masking stimulus: it had the function of erasing the letter array from iconic store; the subject could therefore only carry out the pattern-recognition process during the time that the string of letters was physically present.

The results of this experiment are shown in Figure 2.17. Up to about 40–50 milliseconds, about one letter can be reported for every 10 milliseconds of

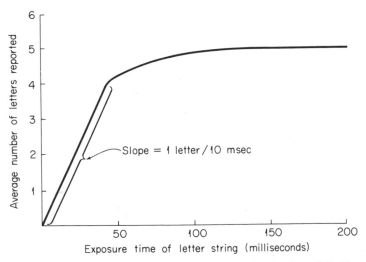

FIGURE 2.17   Results of Sperling's (1963) experiment. (After Sperling, 1963, Figure 5.)

1. Present from 6 to 12 arrays of letters at times varying from 5 to 320 milliseconds per array.

H	D	M
R	F	P
W	C	J

L	X	G
F	H	W
V	C	P

V	N	K
R	M	J
G	T	7

. . .

G	R	L
E	J	F
T	Z	N

Digit embedded in one
location of one array

2. Subject attempts to report location of digit within the array.

FIGURE 2.18   Procedure used in the Sperling *et al.* (1971) experiment.

stimulus presentation time. It therefore appears that in this experiment, the time taken to pattern recognize one letter is 10 milliseconds, or a hundredth of a second, which is very fast. Why does the function level off? Two possibilities exist. The first possibility is that short-term store can only hold about four or five letters and so short-term store quickly becomes filled. The second possibility is that the pattern-recognition process works in "bursts"—that is, the program can operate for only about 100 milliseconds but then needs a rest before it can operate again.

Sperling's second experiment bears on this question. This experiment (Sperling, Budiansky, Spivak, & Johnson, 1971) is illustrated in Figure 2.18. It went as follows: during a given trial in the experiment, the subject saw a series of from six to twelve arrays of letters flashed sequentially on a cathode-ray screen in front of him. (A cathode-ray screen is similar to a television screen.) The catch was that one location of one of the arrays contained not a letter, but a digit. It was the subject's job to report which location contained the digit. The amount of time each array was left on before being replaced by the subsequent array is termed the *interstimulus interval*. In this experiment, the interstimulus interval varied from 5 to 320 milliseconds.

Sperling *et al.* (1971) assumed that when a particular array appeared, the subject began "scanning" the items in the array in an attempt to determine which, if any, of the locations contained the digit. By "scanning" is simply meant pattern recognizing the items one by one. Using the probability that the subject correctly reported the position of the digit, it was possible to estimate how many items had been pattern recognized from each array. Suppose, for example, that this probability were 0.67. We could then infer that the subject has pattern recognized two-thirds of the items in each array, or six out of the nine items in the array.

Figure 2.19 shows the estimated number of items scanned as a function of the interstimulus interval. There are several interesting characteristics of these data. First, notice that when arrays are presented for 40 milliseconds apiece, the subject is estimated to pattern recognize about five items from each array. At this interstimulus interval, therefore, the subject is scanning about one

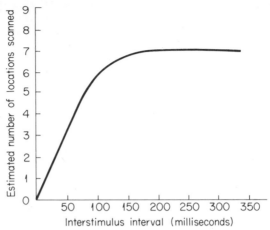

FIGURE 2.19 Results of the Sperling *et al.* (1971) experiment. (After Sperling *et al.*, 1971, Figure 2. Copyright 1971 by the American Association for the Advancement of Science.)

symbol every 8 milliseconds, which agrees quite closely with the estimate of one symbol per 10 milliseconds obtained from Sperling's earlier experiment. The second noteworthy aspect of the data is that the function in Figure 2.19 flattens out in a manner similar to that of the curve in Figure 2.17. Once again, increasing exposure time (interstimulus interval) beyond a certain point does not seem to lead to further pattern recognition of the patterns in the stimulus array. In this experiment, note that the subject was not required to remember the symbols he was pattern recognizing (as his only task was to find the digit). Therefore, he has no need to fill up short-term memory. This reasoning seems to suggest that the levelings off of the curves in Figures 2.17 and 2.19 are not caused by a limit on short-term memory capacity but by a limit on how long the pattern-recognition program can operate before it needs a rest.

Which information is transferred out of sensory store?   Imagine that you have a food freezer that you have just stocked with meat. Suddenly, your city is struck with a power failure that, according to news reports, is going to last for a week or so. Now you are in trouble, for you have a freezer full of meat and, without electricity, meat does not last very long. An obvious course of action in this situation is to have yourself a quick feast. However, because the capacity of your stomach is smaller than the capacity of your freezer, you are then forced to make a choice about which meat you transfer from the freezer to your stomach and which meat you allow to decay away.

An analogous situation occurs when information is to be transferred from sensory store to short-term store. Sensory store can hold a good deal more information than can short-term store. Therefore, a person must make a choice about which information is to be transferred to short-term store and which is left to decay away from sensory store.

Attention.   In deciding which information to transfer, you are essentially deciding to what you are going to attend. In turn, this choice is most likely dictated by the task you are trying to accomplish. Subjects in Sperling's partial report procedure, for example, had to report all the letters from a particular, designated row of the letter array. A high tone signaled the subject to *attend to* the top row and to begin pattern recognizing the top row letters at the expense of the middle and bottom row letters.

The cocktail party phenomenon.   A typical, real-life situation in which the process of attention is demonstrated quite vividly is a crowded, noisy cocktail party. Suppose you are sitting in the middle of such a party with one conversation going on to your right and, simultaneously, another conversation taking place on your left. Both conversations are impinging on your sense organs, so both enter sensory store (in this case, echoic store, as the information is auditory). However, you cannot pay attention to both conversations at once; you can only attend to one. In terms of the information processing system we have been discussing, this means that of all the information in echoic store, you are only pattern recognizing a portion of it (corresponding to the conversation on your right, say) and transferring only this portion of the information to short-term store where it can be processed further. By "processed further" is meant such things as understanding the words in the conversation, possibly making inferences or drawing conclusions from the conversation, memorizing parts of the conversation, and so on.

Dichotic listening experiments.   Psychologists have done experiments to examine the fate of attended versus nonattended information in situations such as the one we have just described. The experiments are not done at an actual cocktail party, because at a cocktail party it is hard to control all of the relevant variables. Instead, the experiments are done in a laboratory using a paradigm called *dichotic listening*. In a dichotic listening task, the subject wears earphones connected to a stereo tape recorder. One message is played to the subject through the left earphone, and simultaneously a completely different message is played through the other earphone. The subject is then required to attend to one message or the other. To insure that the subject attends to the message he is supposed to attend to, he is asked to *shadow* the attended message. Shadowing simply means repeating the message back aloud as it is being presented.

In this sort of situation, the subject processes remarkably little of the information on the nonattended message. Figure 2.20 shows examples of typical dichotic listening experiments, along with the results obtained in such experiments. Cherry (1953), for example, has switched languages on the nonattended channel. The nonattended message started in English, switched to French in the middle, and then switched back to English again. When asked what the language on the nonattended channel has been, subjects have replied

A. Attended message: Subject shadows normal English.
    Nonattended message: Language switches from English to French then back to English.

    Task: After the end of the messages subject is asked the language of the non-
    attended message.
    Result: Subject does not know that the language switched.

B. Attended message: Subject shadows normal message.
    Nonattended message: Short list of words is repeated 35 times.
    Task: At the end of the message, subject is asked to recognize the words on the
    repeated list.
    Result: Subject cannot recognize the words.

C. Attended message: Subject shadows normal message.
    Nonattended message: Normal message.

    Task: Subject is abruptly stopped while shadowing and asked to recall all he can
    of the nonattended message.
    Result: Subject can recall the last few words of the nonattended message.

FIGURE 2.20   Types of dichotic listening experiments.

that they were not sure, but "assumed that it was English throughout." Likewise, Moray (1959) has repeated a short list of words 35 times on the nonattended channel. Later, subjects have not only been unable to recall these words, they could not even recognize them.

Such results indicate that an extraordinarily small amount of processing is done on the information in the nonattended channel. However, in another dichotic listening experiment, subjects were suddenly and unexpectedly stopped in the midst of shadowing and asked to recall all they could from the unattended message. In this situation, the subjects were able to report back the last few things that had been on the unattended channel.

Taken together, these dichotic listening data fit in very nicely with the notion of a fast-decaying echoic store in which nonattended information gets relatively little processing. The results of the first two experiments indicate that nonattended information (that is, information not transferred out of iconic store into short-term store) decays away and is therefore not remembered. However, the results of the third experiment indicate that if requested to a person can almost instantly switch processing and pattern recognize the information residing in another part (that is, the nonattended channel) of echoic store.

SUMMARY

We have started our exploration of the memory system by noting that information from the environment is first placed into sensory store, and we have described a number of characteristics of this store.

1.   Sensory store holds a large amount of information—essentially all the information impinging on a given sense organ.

2. Information in sensory store takes the form of raw, sensory patterns as yet unanalyzed for meaning.

3. Information decays from sensory store very quickly.

4. A portion of the information in sensory store is transferred out via the process of pattern recognition. Pattern recognition is the process of attaching meaning to a sensory pattern and probably consists of testing for the presence or absence of elementary sensory features. The decision of which information to transfer out of sensory store and which to let decay away is the phenomenon of attention.

3
Short-Term Store

We ended Chapter 2 discussing how, via the process of pattern recognition, information is transferred from sensory store to short-term store. In this chapter, we shall be discussing short-term store itself, dealing with the issues of how information is *forgotten* from short-term store, how *much* information can be held in short-term store, the *form* in which information is represented in short-term store, and the processes by which information is *retrieved* from short-term store. Before we discuss these issues, however, we must provide the rationale for why such a concept as short-term store should be included in a theory of memory to begin with.

RATIONALE FOR A DICHOTOMOUS MEMORY

It was William James, writing in the late nineteenth century, who originated the idea that memory consists of two separate components. In James' *dichotomous view* of memory, the first component, or *primary memory* (analogous to what is currently called short-term store), was seen as containing that material which has not yet left consciousness. *Secondary memory* (analogous to what we currently call long-term store), in contrast, was seen as containing material not in consciousness but which is available to be brought into consciousness if needed.

James' dichotomous view is intuitively appealing. Introspectively, it *seems* to us that we have these two types of memory. However, science frowns on notions based only in intuition and demands that a hypothesis be supported by scientific evidence if it is to survive. For a long time after James formulated his dichotomous memory hypothesis, there were no real data to support it; the idea therefore whithered away, and emerging theories took the converse point of view—that memory is *unitary* as opposed to dichotomous.

In the 1950s this situation began to change as some rather striking findings turned up that favored a dichotomous view of memory. We shall discuss two classes of findings: the first class of findings comes out of the laboratory, whereas the second class originates in a clinical setting.

Laboratory evidence: Free recall.   The most convincing experimental evidence for a dichotomous view of memory stems from a paradigm called *free recall*. Figure 3.1 shows how this paradigm works. A free-recall experiment is divided into a study phase and a test phase. In the study phase, a subject is read a list of unrelated words, one at a time. In the test phase, which immediately follows the study phase, the subject is asked simply to recall back as many of the words as possible, in any order. Figure 3.2 shows the result of a typical free-recall experiment (for example, Murdock, 1962). The curve in Figure 3.2 is called a *serial position curve* and is a graph relating the probability of recalling a word to the word's *serial input position*. By "serial input position" is meant the first word read during the study phase, the second word read, and so on up to the last word read. As you can easily see, the probability of recalling a word is strongly dependent on where in the study list the word occurs. Words from the beginning of the list have a relatively high probability of being recalled (this is called the *primacy effect*) and similarly, words from the end of the list have a relatively high probability of being recalled (this is called the *recency effect*). In contrast, words from the middle of the list have a relatively low probability of being recalled.

The reasons that words from the beginning of the list are recalled well are fairly complex and are discussed in Chapter 4. Let us concern ourselves here with the recency effect. Proponents of a unitary view of memory offer the following explanation of the recency effect: the closer a word is to the end of the list, the more recently it has been studied. The more recently it has been studied, the less likely it is that the word has been forgotten. Therefore, words closest to the end of the list are recalled the best. Proponents of a dichotomous view explain the recency effect much differently. The claim that the closer a word is to the end of the list, the higher is its probability of being in short-term store when recall begins, and words that are still in short-term store are recalled perfectly.

I.   Study phase: Experimenter reads a list of words to the subject, one word at a time.

SOAP – OXYGEN – MAPLE – SPIDER – DAISY – BEER – DANCE – CIGAR – BUICK – MARS – MOUNTAIN – BOMB – FINGER – CHAIR – PUPPET

II.   Test Phase: Subject attempts to recall as many of the words as he can in any order.

"CHAIR. . . BOMB. . . SOAP. . . MAPLE. . . ummmm. . . DAISY. . . ummmmmmm. . ."

FIGURE 3.1   Design of a typical free-recall experiment.

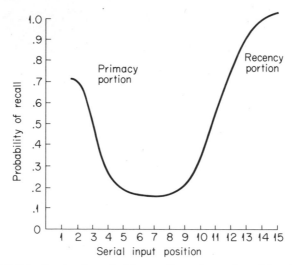

FIGURE 3.2   Results of a typical free-recall experiment: the serial-position curve.

How are we to distinguish between these two views? Suppose we do the following: after the study phase of a free-recall experiment, we do not allow the subject to immediately begin recalling the words. Instead, the subject spends 30 seconds doing a difficult mental arithmetic task and *then* attempts to recall the words. The arithmetic condition can then be compared with a normal control condition in which recall is attempted immediately after the list is read. The unitary and dichotomous views of memory now make quite different predictions about what happens. Figure 3.3a shows the prediction of a unitary view. According to this view, the 30 seconds of arithmetic increases the time between

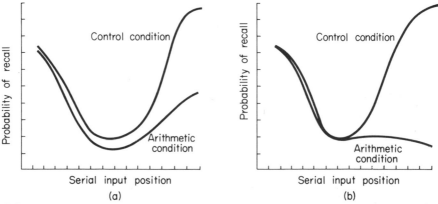

FIGURE 3.3   Predictions of two views of memory in a modified free-recall experiment: (a) unitary view; (b) dichotomous view.

study and test for all words in the list. Therefore, all words in the list have a greater chance to be forgotten and are recalled more poorly than words in the control condition. In the arithmetic condition, however, words from the end of the list should be recalled no better than words from the middle of the list. Moreover, the arithmetic task should have no effect on information that has already been transferred to long-term store, so words from the beginning and middle of the list should be unaffected by the arithmetic. This experiment has been done in two independent laboratories by Postman and Phillips (1965) and by Glanzer and Cunitz (1966). The results of both these studies are very clear-cut: the data can be represented by curves that look like curves in Figure 3.3b. This, then, is evidence favoring the dichotomization of memory into two separate stores.

The logic of this demonstration rests on the fact that a particular experimental variable (in this case, doing versus not doing the arithmetic task) affects one portion but not the other of the serial position curve. This general finding provides nice support for the claim that the two portions of the curve are based on information coming from two different memory stores. The Glanzer–Cunitz and Postman–Phillips experiments have demonstrated a variable that affects the recency but not the primacy portion of the curve. In an analogous fashion, other experiments have demonstrated that there are variables affecting the primacy but not the recency portion; some of these variables are illustrated in Figure 3.4. First, if words are varied in terms of presentation rate, faster

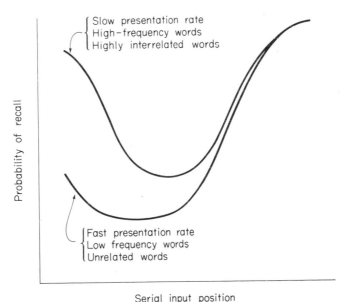

FIGURE 3.4   Experimental variables that affect the primacy but not the recency portion of the serial-position curve.

presented words show poorer primacy than slower presented words (Glanzer & Cunitz, 1966). Second, words with high frequency in the language, such as "dog" or "table," show better primacy than low-frequency words, such as "microbe" or "legacy" (Sumby, 1963). Finally, if the list is made up of highly interrelated words, such as "black," "white," "table," and "chair," there is better primacy than if the words are not interrelated (Glanzer & Schwartz, 1971). In all of these studies, variables that strongly affect the recency portion of the serial-position curve leave the primacy portion untouched, again supporting the notion that the information on which the two portions of the curve are based is held in two different memory stores. The variables shown in Figure 3.4 apparently affect long-term store but have no effects on short-term store.

Clinical evidence: The strange case of H. M.   In 1954, a Montreal neuropsychologist, Brenda Milner, had a patient whom she referred to in her writings (Milner, 1966) as "H. M." (the patient's initials). H. M. originally had a severe case of epilepsy, and it was believed that by removing a certain portion of H. M.'s brain (the hippocampus) the epilepsy could be cured. As it turned out, the operation was successful in that the epilepsy was, in fact, cured. Following the operation, H. M. was given a battery of tests designed to detect any potentially harmful side effects. In terms of memory performance, H. M. had no trouble recalling events that had taken place or things he had learned before the operation. He knew his name, his address, the multiplication table; he remembered World War II, and so on. Likewise, H. M. had no more trouble than anyone else remembering limited amounts of information (such as telephone numbers) for short periods of time, and as could anyone else, he could maintain such information indefinitely by rehearsing it. However, a bizarre malady soon became apparent: H. M. could not learn anything new! For example, if a doctor came into H. M.'s room, H. M. could be introduced to him and carry on a fairly normal conversation. However, if the doctor left the room and returned 5 minutes later, H. M. would have no recollection of ever having seen him before.

H. M.'s case provides fairly compelling evidence for two distinct memory stores. In terms of the memory framework we have been discussing, H. M.'s long-term store is perfectly intact; this is indicated by the fact that he has no trouble retrieving information that had been placed into long-term store prior to the operation. Likewise, H. M.'s short-term store is perfectly intact, for he has no trouble remembering limited amounts of information for short periods of time. However, the operation seems to have destroyed whatever mechanism is responsible for transferring information from short- to long-term store.

Similar, but somewhat more systematic, observations have been made in England by Baddeley and Warrington (1970). Baddeley and Warrington worked with a group of patients who had memory deficits similar to that of H. M., comparing these patients to normal (nonamnesic) control subjects in a series of standard memory tests. Again, the majority of evidence indicated that the patients' rehearsal and short-term memory functioning were quite normal; however, when the patients were asked to remember information that they had received more than a few seconds previously, their performance was, in most cases, poorer than that of the normal controls.

It should be emphasized that in these clinical studies, the evidence for the short-term memory–long-term memory dichotomy comes from the fact that some aspects of the patients' memory functioning is quite normal, whereas other aspects are impaired. The conclusion is that the normal functioning must be based on information in one memory store whereas the impaired functioning must be based on information in another memory store.

FORGETTING FROM SHORT-TERM STORE

In Chapter 1, it is noted that unrehearsed information is forgotten from short-term store quite rapidly. Intuitively, this makes sense. Suppose I look up a number in the telephone directory and then walk across the room to dial it. If I do not rehearse the number as I am walking, chances are that I shall have forgotten it by the time I reach the telephone. Exactly how long does it take for information to be forgotten from short-term store? This question has been investigated by Brown in 1958 and by Peterson and Peterson (a husband–wife team) in 1959.

The Brown–Peterson paradigm. The Brown–Peterson paradigm is quite straightforward and is shown on the left-hand side of Figure 3.5. Each trial in the experiment begins with the insertion of some information, for example a consonant trigram, into the subject's short-term store. (A *consonant trigram* is simply a string of three consonants, such as GKB.) Following presentation of the trigram is a variable *retention interval* ranging, for example, from 0 to 18 seconds. In order to prevent rehearsal of the trigram during

Experimental procedure	What is assumed to be happening in the subject's head
I. Subject reads a consonent trigram (e.g., GKB) for 2 seconds.	I. Information corresponding to GKB is put into the subject's short-term store. A small amount of information is transferred to long-term store.
II. Variable retention interval (0-18 seconds). Subject counts backward by threes to prevent rehearsal of GKB.	II. Information is forgotten from short-term store.
III. Subject attempts to recall the trigram.	III. Recall can be based either on information in short-term store or on information in long-term store.

FIGURE 3.5   The Brown–Peterson forgetting paradigm.

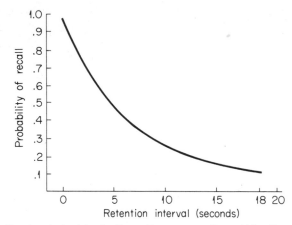

FIGURE 3.6   Results obtained in the Brown-Peterson paradigm. (After Peterson & Peterson, 1959, Figure 3. Copyright 1959 by the American Psychological Association. Reproduced by permission.)

the retention interval, the subject is required to perform a difficult mental arithmetic task (counting backward by threes from a three-digit number) during the interval. At the end of the interval, the amount of information left in the subject's short-term store is measured by asking the subject to recall the trigram and seeing how often he is able to do it.

Figure 3.6 shows the results obtained in the Brown–Peterson paradigm. Here, the probability of recalling the trigram is shown as a function of the length of the retention interval. If the trigram is tested immediately (that is, at a retention interval of zero) then recall performance is virtually perfect. At longer retention invervals, memory performance drops rapidly until at an interval of about 15 seconds, the trigram is only recalled about 10% of the time. At intervals longer than 15 seconds, memory performance does not drop any further; it remains at a 10% asymptotic level.

The right-hand side of Figure 3.5 depicts what is assumed to be happening in this paradigm. Consider first the period during which the trigram is initially presented. At this time, information about the trigram is placed into short-term store; additionally, this 2 seconds is sufficient time for a small amount of information about the trigram to be transferred from short-term store to long-term store. During the retention interval, information is lost from short-term store, this forgetting being complete in about 15 seconds. At intervals longer than 15 seconds, responses must be based on the (meager) information that has been transferred to long-term store. As we can see from the data in Figure 3.5, this information is apparently sufficient to allow the subject to respond correctly about 10% of the time.

What causes forgetting from short-term store?   The results of the Brown–Peterson paradigm demonstrate that forgetting from short-term store is complete within about 15 seconds. What processes are responsible for this forgetting? In order for forgetting to take place, the subject must perform some intervening activity, such as an arithmetic task, to prevent rehearsal; short-term forgetting therefore certainly depends on events occurring *following* the storage of information. However, as we shall see in the next section, short-term forgetting also depends on events occurring *prior to* the storage of information.

In attempting to account for the rapid short-term forgetting found by Brown and by Peterson and Peterson, it has been hypothesized that perhaps information the subject is currently trying to remember is interfered with by other information stored earlier. To investigate this hypothesis, Keppel and Underwood (1962) have replicated the Brown–Peterson experiment but have concerned themselves only with what happens in the first few trials of the experiment. In the Keppel–Underwood experiment, a subject walked into the laboratory, was given three trials of the sort shown in Figure 3.5, and was then dismissed. Let us now plot the forgetting curve shown in Figure 3.6 for the first, second, and third trials. The results of such a procedure are shown in Figure 3.7 and are striking indeed. On Trial 1, no forgetting occurs! Even after an interval of 18 seconds, the subject is still able to recall the trigram virtually perfectly. On Trial 2, some forgetting occurs, and by Trial 3, the forgetting curve looks about like the one shown in Figure 3.5. The depressing influence that

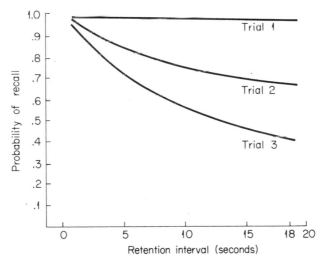

FIGURE 3.7   The Brown-Peterson curve plotted for the first, second, and third trials: results of the Keppel–Underwood (1962) experiment. (Adapted from Keppel & Underwood, 1962.)

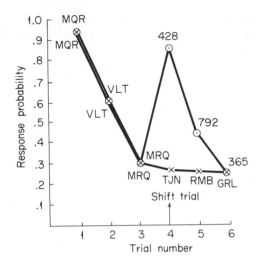

FIGURE 3.8 The "release from proactive interference" paradigm used by Wickens (hypothetical results): (o) Experimental group; (×) control group. An example of the stimuli used is shown above each point for the experimental group and below each point for the control group. The experimental group shifts stimuli on Trial 4.

the first few trials seem to exert on subsequent trial performance has been labeled *proactive interference*.

Keppel and Underwood's finding of short-term proactive interference has been replicated and extended by Delos Wickens and his colleagues (Wickens, Born, & Allen, 1963; Wickens, 1970, 1972). The major contribution of these studies has been to show that in order for proactive interference to operate, it is not sufficient that the subject has just tried to recall material; additionally, the prior information must be in some way *similar* to the information the subject is currently trying to remember. Figure 3.8 illustrates the sort of experiment used by Wickens to demonstrate this fact. Retention interval is held constant (in the example, at 15 seconds). One group of subjects (the control group) receives six trials using consonant trigrams as stimuli. A second (experimental) group receives three trials using consonant trigrams, but on the fourth trial, the study material is swtiched—instead of stimuli consisting of three letters, the stimuli for Trials 4, 5, and 6 consist of three digits. The results of this procedure are quite dramatic: the switching of study material on Trial 4 leads to a substantial increase in performance. After three trials with the new material, performance in the experimental condition has dropped to the point where it is again comparable to performance in the control group. Apparently, if a subject is trying to remember letters, forgetting depends on his just previously having tried to remember other letters; if he is trying to remember digits, forgetting depends on his just previously having tried to remember other digits.

The phenomenon of proactive interference and Wickens' related "release from proactive interference" suggests that short-term forgetting is caused at least in part by interference from prior information. The process by which this interference operates is not clear; the most reasonable explanation seems to be that the information corresponding to prior items may *compete* with information corresponding to the current trigram in terms of which information is chosen by the subject as the basis for his response. Such a competition notion is supported by the fact that when the subject makes an error in a Peterson–Peterson experiment, it is often a *prior item intrusion*, that is, some information from a previous trial. An experiment by G. R. Loftus and Patterson (1975) has strengthened the competition notion by showing that more recently processed information is more likely to intrude than less recently processed information.

CAPACITY OF SHORT-TERM STORE

Up to now we have been asserting that short-term store is of small capacity. In this section, we shall be more precise about this issue and discuss what exactly short-term store capacity is and how it is measured.

To deal with this question, we first need a unit of measurement. As we have noted in Chapter 1, if we want to measure the capacity of a bathtub or a thimble or a cement truck, we can do so in terms of quarts or cubic centimeters or whatever. What is an appropriate unit with which to measure memory capacity? Because we have been talking about "information" as the stuff that fills up memory, an appropriate candidate for such a unit of measurement may be a *bit*. That is, the first hypothesis to test is that short-term store holds some constant number of bits of information.

Tests of short-term store capacity: Memory-span experiments. One way of measuring short-term store capacity is via a memory-span procedure. Such a procedure is quite simple and is often used as part of IQ tests. A subject is read a string of items (for example, a string of digits, such as 7323965) and is then required to repeat back as many of them as he can remember. The experiment begins with some rather small number of items in the string (for example, two digits) and the number of items is then increased until the subject begins to make errors when repeating them back. The capacity of short-term store is then defined as the maximum number of items the subject can repeat back perfectly.

Suppose now that we perform such memory-span experiments using different types of items. If it is indeed the case that short-term store holds some constant amount of information, then the number of items the subject can hold in his short-term store should systematically depend on what the items are. Figure 3.9 illustrates why this is so. Imagine that the capacity of short-term store is 10 bits

Binary digits:	Bit 1	Bit 2	Bit 3	Bit 4	Bit 5	Bit 6	Bit 7	Bit 8	Bit 9	Bit 10
(1 bit per item)	0	1	1	0	0	1	0	1	1	0

Letters:	Bits 1–5	Bits 6–10
(5 bits per item)	A	X

Binary digits	Letters
11	SL
010	NTQ
1011	WPSB
01001	MSEUT
111010	DTOINL
0100010	WDPCFPG
10101100	TMSONWCR
010010011	CTHDAIASL
1111010010	TINCPBNWSE

FIGURE 3.9 Predictions about the outcome of memory span experiments assuming that short-term store holds 10 bits.

and imagine that two memory span experiments are done, one using strings of binary digits (which are 1's and 0's and which contain 1 bit per item) and the other using strings of letters (which contain about 5 bits per item). We should then find that our subject's 10-bit memory should be able to hold ten binary digits at 1 bit per digit, but only two letters at 5 bits per letter.

For your convenience, random strings of binary digits and letters are included in Figure 3.9 so you can try this procedure with a friend if you wish. If you do so, you are likely to find that your friend is able to remember about seven items, whether the items are binary digits or letters. Notice that this means that short-term store can apparently hold only 7 bits of information when the information is in the form of binary digits, but it can hold about 30 bits of information when the information is in the forms of letters!

Hayes (1952) and Pollack (1953) have carried out the memory-span procedure using many different kinds of stimuli. Figure 3.10 shows the result of such a procedure, plotting the number of items a subject can remember as a function of the amount of information in each item. The dashed line in Figure 3.10 shows how the results should appear if short-term memory capacity were constant in terms of bits of information. As discussed above, the more information per item, the smaller the number of items that should be able to fit into short-term store. The actual results are shown by the solid line in Figure 3.10. As you can see, it turns out that a subject is able to remember around seven items, no matter how much information is contained in each item.

Chunks.   The results of these memory-span experiments indicate that the capacity of short-term store is constant, but in a very strange sort of way: short-term store seems to be able to hold about seven of anything! In 1956, George Miller wrote a classic paper entitled "The magical number seven, plus or minus two" in which he coined the word "chunk" to denote that of which

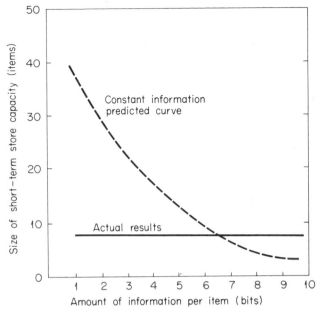

FIGURE 3.10   Memory span as a function of the amount of information per item. (After Miller, 1956. Copyright 1956 by the American Psychological Association. Reproduced by permission.)

short-term store can hold about seven. Exactly what a "chunk" is, alas, is, somewhat ill defined but it might best be characterized as anything that has some unitary representation in long-term store. For example, a digit, such as "5," is a chunk. So is a letter, such as "G," or a word, such as "clown." Going somewhat further, even a proverb such as "Too many cooks spoil the broth" can be thought of as a chunk because a proverb, like a digit or a letter or a word, has a unitary representation in long-term store. It can therefore be expected that in a memory-span experiment, a subject is able to remember about seven proverbs.

Recoding schemes.   One consequence of this finding is that a person must be able to vastly improve his short-term store capacity by judiciously *recoding* many low-information chunks into fewer high-information chunks. Imagine, for example, that a person is trying to remember strings of binary digits. As we have seen, under ordinary circumstances, each binary digit corresponds to one chunk; therefore a person is able to hold about seven binary digits in short-term store. Suppose, however, that the person has craftily memorized the recoding scheme depicted in Figure 3.11. In this recoding scheme, a given string of four binary digits is recoded into some particular letter. Therefore, our subject listening to a long string of binary digits, for example, 010110010111 . . . , can recode each group of four binary digits into

String of binary digits	Letter
0000 ──────────→	A
0001 ──────────→	B
0010 ──────────→	C
0011 ──────────→	D
0100 ──────────→	E
0101 ──────────→	F
0110 ──────────→	G
0111 ──────────→	H
1000 ──────────→	I
1001 ──────────→	J
1010 ──────────→	K
1011 ──────────→	L
1100 ──────────→	M
1101 ──────────→	N
1110 ──────────→	O
1111 ──────────→	P

FIGURE 3.11 A possible recoding scheme for increasing the memory span for binary digits.

its corresponding letter, that is FJH. . . . How many binary digits can now be remembered? We know that the subject can remember about seven letters; and because each letter corresponds to four binary digits, he can now remember about 7 × 4 = 28, which is quite an improvement over seven! A fellow named Smith (reported by Miller, 1956) was able to remember strings of 40 binary digits using similar recoding schemes. Such schemes form the basis of many of the "miraculously improve your memory" courses that you see advertised from time to time in Sunday-supplement magazine sections.

Lest you think that recoding schemes are used only by "memory experts" and psychologists, let us hasten to point out that they are used by all people, all the time, in everyday life. Suppose I give you the five words FORT, BAND, SOCK, TRIP, and CARD to remember. Probably, you have no trouble keeping these five words in your short-term store. However, notice that at the same time you are also maintaining 20 letters in your short-term store (since each of the five words is composed of four letters). How is this to be reconciled with the fact that only seven letters can, in general, be maintained in short-term store? The answer is that only seven letters can be held when the letters are *unrelated* to one another. Organizing four letters into a word, however, is a recoding scheme much like the one shown in Figure 3.4. Just as we can learn a recoding scheme that welds four binary digit chunks, such as 1001, into the informationally richer letter chunk J, we have learned the recoding scheme that welds the four letter chunks, F, O, R, and T into the informationally richer word chunk, FORT. A fairly common parlor trick illustrates the notion of a recoding scheme quite dramatically. Tell a person that you will read 12 letters and that you want him to repeat back as many of the letters as possible in the correct order. Then read the following letters grouped in the following way: FB–ITW–AC–IAIB–M. Chances are that the person will not be able to remember very many of the letters. Now read exactly the same letters to another person, but grouped slightly differently: FBI–TWA–CIA–IBM. You are now likely to find that your lucky subject remembers all 12 letters. Why the improvement? Again, the answer is in the terms of chunks. In the first instance, there were 12 unrelated letters, that is, 12 chunks, which is well beyond the memory span. In the second instance, there are only four chunks, because a letter triad, such as FBI, is represented in a unitary way—encoded as a single chunk—in long-term store. Because four chunks is considerably less than short-term store capacity, they can all be held in short-term store and then recalled.

Before we leave the topic of short-term store capacity, it may be useful to provide a computer analogy of what is going on; this analogy is illustrated in Figure 3.12. Here, a computer is seen as having seven special memory locations designated "short-term store." Additionally, the computer has a vast number of other memory locations that correspond to long-term store. Figure 3.12a shows what happens when our computer is given a list of words to remember. Suppose the first word is "HOMEWORK." The computer puts into the first short-term store slot not the actual word, HOMEWORK, but a *pointer* to the location in long-term store where the word HOMEWORK is stored. The computer does the same thing for the second word (LUNCH) and

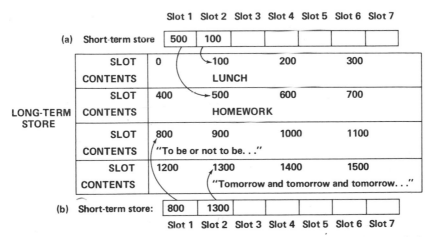

FIGURE 3.12 Computer analogy of short-term store: (a) remembering words; (b) remembering Shakespeare soliloquies.

so on until the seven short-term store slots are filled with pointers to appropriate long-term store locations. Notice that with this method, the computer can store seven chunks "in short-term store" no matter how complex the chunks are. To take matters to extremes, Figure 3.12b assumes that our computer is a Shakespeare buff and has memorized Shakespeare soliloquies. Each soliloquy is then stored in long-term store as a single chunk, and the computer, by using the pointer technique, is able to store seven soliloquies "in short-term store" in exactly the same fashion as it stored seven words "in short-term store."

FORM OF INFORMATION STORED IN SHORT-TERM STORE

We have noted in Chapter 2 that the physical representation of information in sensory store takes the form of a faithful reflection of the original stimulus. Information in echoic store is auditory, whereas information in iconic store is visual. In this section, we shall present evidence that when raw, sensory information is pattern recognized and placed into short-term store, its representation there is basically auditory. Like many other hypotheses we have discussed, the hypothesis of auditory information storage in short-term store makes sense from an intuitive or introspective point of view. Consider, for example, a letter string, such as LEJF. Look away from this page and hold this letter string in your short-term store—that is, rehearse it to yourself and introspect about what is happening. If you are like most people, your rehearsal consists of successively repeating the letters to yourself with your "mind's voice" and hearing the resulting spoken representation in your "mind's ear." This is equivalent to saying that you are maintaining an auditory representation of the letters in short-term store. Later, we shall present a more formal model of what this process involves in order to lend some scientific respectability to these intuitive speculations. First, however, we shall discuss some laboratory data favoring an auditory representation of information in short-term store.

Errors.   Suppose a subject is given some information (such as a string of letters) to maintain in short-term store. As we have seen in previous sections, there are various circumstances under which the subject makes errors when attempting to recall the information. We can overload memory capacity (say, by giving the subject ten chunks to try to remember) or we can force the subject to perform a complex mental task (such as counting backward by threes) which causes him to forget some of the information. In either case, the hypothesis of an auditory representation of information in short-term store leads to some rather specific predictions about what the nature of the errors is. Let us work through these predictions.

An auditory representation of a particular letter can be thought of as consisting of several auditory *features* (which linguists call *phonemes*). For example, the letter "B" consists of the initial "beh" phoneme, plus the final "eee" phoneme. Likewise, the letter "F" consists of an initial "ehh" plus a final "fff" and the letter "K" has an initial "k" plus a final "ay." Suppose now we present the letter trigram, "BFK" in a Peterson–Peterson forgetting trial and that a given letter is forgotten phoneme by phoneme (a scheme proposed by Sperling & Speelman, 1970). Focusing on the letter "B," one of four things may happen. First, neither of the two phonemes may be forgotten. In this case, the letter is recalled with no problem. At the other extreme, both phonemes may be forgotten. If this happens, the subject either omits the letter altogether or guesses randomly from the 26 letters of the alphabet. The third possibility is that only the final "eee" phoneme is forgotten, in which case the initial "beh" still provides the subject with enough information to recall the B (because no other letter in the alphabet contains the phoneme "beh" and our clever subject is thereby able to figure out that B must be the correct answer). Finally, the initial "beh" may be forgotten. In this case, only the final "eee" remains, and the subject is forced to guess randomly among and output one of the letters B, C, D, E, G, P, T, V, and Z that end in "eee."

Similar arguments can be made for the letters F and K. For F, if an error is made, it will probably be one of the letters L, M, N, S, or X (the letters that begin with the phoneme "ehh"). Likewise, if an error is made for K, it is likely to be A or J (which contain an "ay" phoneme). In short, the hypothesis of auditory information storage predicts that errors made out of short-term store bear an *acoustic relationship* to the correct information.

This prediction has been confirmed in a variety of experiments. First, R. Conrad (1964) has found that errors are acoustically related to correct responses in a memory-span experiment. For example, given the letter string ACQFGHJP, the subject may substitute a T for the C and recall ATQFGHJP. Second, in the Brown–Peterson paradigm, errors tend to be acoustically related to correct responses at short but not at long retention intervals (R. Conrad, 1967; Estes, 1972, 1973; Bjork & Healy, 1974). Again this follows from the analysis presented above: at short retention intervals, chances are that only one phoneme is forgotten, so the subject guesses on the basis of partial acoustic information and makes an acoustic error. At long retention intervals, however, all phonemes are forgotten, and guesses are random. Finally, experiments by R. Conrad and Hull (1964) and by Wickelgren (1965) have presented subjects with strings of letters that are either acoustically similar (for example, EGCZDBG) or acoustically dissimilar (for example, FGOAYQR). Again, in accordance with the auditory storage hypothesis, performance on the acoustically similar strings is considerably poorer than performance on the acoustically dissimilar strings.

A model for short-term store.   In 1967, a model of short-term store that tied together many of the features we discussed above was proposed by our old

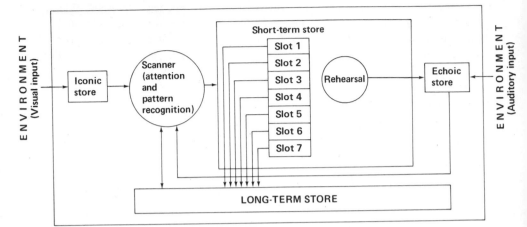

FIGURE 3.13   A model of short-term store. (Adapted from Sperling, 1967.)

friend, the ubiquitous George Sperling. A somewhat reinterpreted version of Sperling's model (which may be viewed as an elaboration of the scheme depicted in Figure 2.15) is shown in Figure 3.13. The model simultaneously incorporates the notions of attention, pattern recognition, limited capacity, rehearsal, and auditory information storage.

The scheme shown in Figure 3.13 may look big and scary and complicated, but it's not. To begin with the large box represents a human, and everything outside the box represents the environment. In accord with our previous discussions, information enters the human either through the eyes (represented by the arrow coming into the left-hand side of the box) or through the ears (represented by the arrow coming into the right-hand side of the box). Visual information goes directly into iconic store, whereas auditory information goes directly into echoic store. Information in either sensory store is processed by a "scanner," which includes both attention (it decides which information to process) and pattern recognition. (Notice that in Figure 3.13, circles *process* information, whereas boxes *hold* information.) The result of the scanner's operation is to fill up seven slots in short-term store with one chunk of information per slot. Recall from the previous section (and Figure 3.12) that it is not the actual information that goes into a particular slot but rather a pointer to the area of long-term store where the actual information resides. This notion is reflected by the arrows in the model connecting each short-term store slot with the appropriate area of long-term store. The next component of the model is a rehearsal process. The rehearsal component, which can be thought of as a "mind's voice," goes successively through each slot creating an auditory representation of the information identified by the slot. The auditory representation then acts as a new auditory stimulus and is placed into echoic store where any auditory stimulus is placed. The scanner then reoperates on echoic store, replacing the information into its appropriate slot, and the information in short-term store is thereby continuously recycled.

RETRIEVAL OF INFORMATION FROM SHORT-TERM STORE

We have been assuming that information residing in short-term store can be retrieved and used rapidly and efficiently. In this section, we shall examine the short-term retrieval process in somewhat more detail.

The Sternberg paradigm. An experimental paradigm that has been extremely useful in examining short-term information retrieval was developed about a decade ago at the Bell Telephone Laboratories by Saul Sternberg (Sternberg, 1966, 1967, 1969a, b). The task used by Sternberg is shown in Figure 3.14. A given trial in this paradigm consists of a storage (study) phase and a retrieval (test) phase. In the storage phase, the subject is read or shown a string of items (for example, digits), which he places in his short-term store. This string of items is referred to as the *memory set*. When the subject is satisfied that he has the memory set in short-term store, he presses a button that initiates the retrieval phase of the trial. In the retrieval phase, a single item (the test item) appears and the subject simply has to report whether the test item was or was not a member of the memory set. In the example shown in Figure 3.14, the memory set consists of the digits 3, 1, 7, and 4. If the test item were, for example, a 1, the correct response would be "Yes," whereas if the test item were, for example a 6, the correct response would be "No." The response is not actually a spoken response, but is made by pressing a button. One button

I.   **Storage phase**

　　A.   Memory set is presented

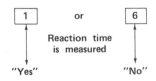

　　B.   Subject enters memory set into short-term store

II. **Retrieval phase**

　　A.   Test digit is presented

　　　　　1   or   6

　　　　　Reaction time
　　　　　is measured

　　　　"Yes"   "No"

　　B.   Response is made

FIGURE 3.14   A trial in the Sternberg (1966) paradigm.

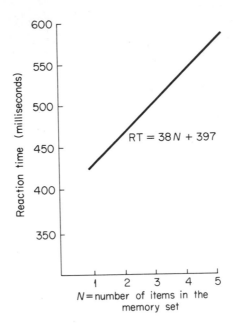

FIGURE 3.15 Results of the Sternberg (1966) experiment. (After Sternberg, 1966, Figure 1. Copyright 1966 by the American Association for the Advancement of Science.)

corresponds to "yes" and a second button corresponds to "no." Subjects are instructed to respond as quickly as possible but to avoid making errors. In practice, the error rate is generally quite low, under 5%, and the dependent variable of interest is the reaction time between the appearance of the test digit and the subject's response.

Is retrieval carried out sequentially or in parallel? Using the Sternberg paradigm, we can investigate a major and basic question about retrieval of information from short-term store: is all the information in short-term store searched in parallel and the desired information simply "plucked out" or is it necessary to search sequentially (item by item)? To answer this question, Sternberg simply varied the amount of information in short-term store—that is, the size of the memory set. By looking at the function relating reaction time to memory set size, we can now distinguish between the parallel and sequential hypotheses. If a parallel search is made of all information in short-term store, then the number of items in short-term store should have a relatively minor effect on search time. Conversely, if information is examined sequentially, then the more items in short-term store to be searched through, the longer the search should take. In other words, the sequential hypothesis predicts that reaction time should increase as a function of memory set size.

Figure 3.15 shows the results of Sternberg's experiments. There are several interesting aspects of these data. First, the fact that the curve rises suggests that a sequential search is being made. Second, the fact that the curve is linear has led Sternberg to postulate a fairly specific model of the retrieval process in terms of *processing stages*.

A sequential search model.   Sternberg postulates that the reaction time to respond is made up of several *independent stages*, each stage taking some amount of time. In particular, the stages are assumed to be roughly as follows:

Stage 1. The test digit is read and encoded (pattern recognized). Assume that this stage takes e milliseconds.

Stage 2. The encoded form of the test digit is successively compared with each member of the memory set. Each comparison consists of a determination of whether a match exists between the test item and the memory set item with which it is being compared. Assume the time to make one comparison takes c milliseconds. If there are N items in the memory set, the total time taken in the comparison stage is therefore cN milliseconds.

Stage 3. Based on whether or not a match was found a decision is made to respond "yes" or "no" and the response is executed. Assume that it takes d milliseconds to make the decision and execute the response.

Adding up the times for these three stages, we find that reaction time (RT) may be expressed by the following equation:

$$RT = \text{Stage 1} + \text{Stage 2} + \text{Stage 3}$$

or

(3.1) $$RT = e + cN + d.$$

The meaning of a linear function.   Recall that the general expression for a linear function relating two variables, x and y, takes the form

$$y = ax + b,$$

Where a is the slope of the function and b is the y intercept of the function. To see how Sternberg's model predicts the linear function of Figure 3.15 relating reaction time and memory set size (N) let us rearrange the terms of Equation (3.1) to get

$$RT = cN + (e + d).$$

Reaction time is therefore predicted to be a linear function of N with a slope equal to c and a y intercept equal to $(e + d)$.

Now, from the data in Figure 3.15, we can calculate the slope c, which is about 38 milliseconds per item, and the intercept $(e + d)$, which is about 397 milliseconds. Putting together the model and the data, we can therefore conclude that it takes about 38 milliseconds to make one comparison and about

397 milliseconds for the combined times of test item encoding, decision making, and response execution.

The astute reader has probably noticed something fishy in the data of Figure 3.15 and is bothered by the question: does the ordinate of the graph represent the time to respond "Yes" or the time to respond "No"? The answer is that *both* yes and no reaction times yield the function shown in Figure 3.15. The fact that yes and no reaction times produce the same function may seem strange for the following reason: in order for a subject to respond "No," he must compare the test item with *every* item in the memory set in order to determine that none of the memory set items matches the test item. It seems, however, that when the test item *is* contained in the memory set (that is, when the correct response is "Yes") the subject typically has to make fewer comparisons, since as soon as a match is found, the search process can be halted and a response made. In fact, because on the average the match is made in the *middle* of the memory set, only half [actually $(N + 1)/2$] of the possible comparisons need be made for a memory set of size N. This type of a *self-terminating* scheme therefore predicts that when a "Yes" response is made, the total time for the comparison stage is $c(N/2)$ or $(c/2)N$ milliseconds. We should therefore find that for "Yes" responses,

$$RT \text{ (yes)} = (c/2)N + (c/2 + e + d),$$

whereas for "No" responses

$$RT \text{ (no)} = cN + (e + d),$$

or the slope of the yes function should be half that of the no function. The fact that the slopes are equal for the two functions indicates, surprisingly, that the subject performs an *exhaustive* search through short-term store as opposed to a self-terminating one. That is, even when a match is found between the test item and one of the memory set items, the subject continues to compare the test item to the rest of the memory set items. Why should the subject use such a seemingly inefficient strategy? The answer to this puzzling question is not really clear. One possibility is that the decision process takes a long time relative to the comparison process. Instead of making a decision following every comparison, it may actually be faster to wait until all the comparisons have been made and then make the decision only once.

To summarize, Sternberg's data have suggested that subjects perform a *sequential exhaustive search* to retrieve information from short-term store. The fact that the reaction time function is a linearly increasing one provides the evidence that the search is sequential (not parallel). Evidence that the search is exhaustive (not self-terminating) is provided by the fact that the yes and no reaction time functions have the same slope. Sternberg's findings are very powerful ones in that they have been replicated many times with various types of stimulus materials and there has been very little variation either in the linear form of the function or in the estimated 30–40 millisecond per item comparison time.

SUMMARY

We began this chapter by describing two lines of evidence supporting a theoretical distinction between short-term and long-term store. First, laboratory evidence stems primarily from the free-recall paradigm. Free-recall experiments have shown that various experimental manipulations affect one part of the serial position curve leaving other parts untouched, suggesting that different portions of the curve reflect information in different memory stores. Analogously, *clinical* evidence has shown cases in which one type of memory function is drastically impaired while at the same time other types of memory function are completely intact.

The major characteristics of short-term store include the following:

1. Forgetting from short-term store is complete in about 15 seconds. Forgetting is also dependent on the subject's just having retrieved information similar to the information he is currently trying to remember.
2. The capacity of short-term store is about seven chunks, where a chunk is anything with a unitary representation in long-term store.
3. Information is represented in an acoustic form in short-term store.
4. Information in short-term store is retrieved via a sequential, exhaustive search.

4
Long-Term Memory for New Material

We are all aware that humans are able to store vast amounts of information—words, names, faces, places—permanently or semipermanently in long-term store. Without long-term store there would be nothing: no books, no television, no learning, no communication—for it is our ability to recall the past that allows us to interact with our environment in a dynamic way. Yet memory ranks high on the list of phenomena about which there are many unanswered questions: how does all this information get into long-term store to begin with? How can information be selectively and almost instantaneously recalled from long-term store when it is needed? Such questions have intrigued philosophers and scientists for more than 2000 years. In this chapter we discuss some of psychology's steps toward answering these and related questions.

ENTRY OF INFORMATION INTO LONG-TERM STORE: REHEARSAL

We note in Chapter 1 that we rehearse information when we repeat it over and over, as when we look up a telephone number in the telephone book and repeat it to ourselves. Rehearsal can do two things: it can keep the information in short-term store for as long as we continue rehearsing, and it can also act as a mechanism by which information is transferred from short-term to long-term store. In terms of the phone number, if we rehearse it enough, we can later retrieve it from the long-term store and we do not have to look it up anymore. Empirical evidence that rehearsal may act as an information-transfer mechanism is provided by several experiments.

Rehearsal in a Brown–Peterson task.   Hellyer (1962) added a new twist to the Brown–Peterson task. He presented a consonant trigram for the subject to study, but on some trials the subject rehearsed the trigram aloud once, whereas on other trials he rehearsed two, four, or eight times. Presentation and rehearsal of the trigram was then followed by a variable retention interval during which the subject engaged in an arithmetic task to prevent further rehearsal.

Figure 4.1 shows Hellyer's results. Notice that in all repetition conditions forgetting takes place. The greater the number of times a trigram is repeated, however, the higher is the asymptotic level of recall. It has been pointed out in Chapter 3 that the asymptote of the retention function is thought to represent performance based on information in long-term store; Hellyer's findings therefore provide direct evidence to suggest that more rehearsal leads to the transfer of more information to long-term store.

Rehearsal and the Hebb paradigm.   A classic experiment by Hebb (1961) gave further support for the notion that rehearsal is involved in the transfer of information to long-term store. On each of 12 trials, a subject in Hebb's experiment was read a nine-digit number, such as 981354762, and then he tried to repeat the number back. What the subject did not know, however, was that on every third trial the *same* string of nine digits was repeated. So the string 981354762 might be presented on Trials 1, 4, 7, and 10. Different nine-digit numbers were used on all of the other trials.

Figure 4.2 shows the results of this procedure: over trials, performance on the new, changing strings does not improve, whereas performance on the repeated, unchanging string improves steadily. The improvement for the unchanging strings suggests that every time a string of numbers is presented,

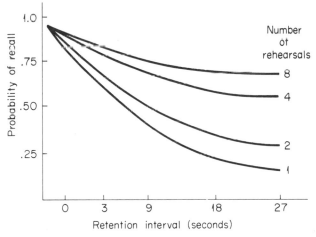

FIGURE 4.1   Results of the Hellyer (1962) experiment. Recall performance as a function of the length of the retention interval for trigrams rehearsed one, two, four, or eight times. (Adapted from Hellyer, 1962.)

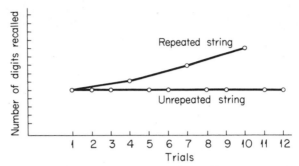

FIGURE 4.2   Results of the Hebb (1961) experiment. Recall improves on strings of numbers that are repeated every third trial. Recall is constant on strings that do not repeat. (After Hebb, 1961, Figure 1. Courtesy of Charles C. Thomas, Publisher, Springfield, Illinois.)

some amount of information about that string enters long-term store; this added information then serves to improve performance on the string the next time it is presented.

Rehearsing aloud: Rundus' free-recall experiments.   A series of experiments by Dewey Rundus (Rundus & Atkinson, 1970; Rundus, Loftus, & Atkinson, 1970; Rundus, 1971) provides another confirmation of the relationship between rehearsal and long-term memory performance. Rundus carried out standard free-recall experiments with a new twist: subjects had to rehearse out loud during the presentation of the lists. A subject was asked to rehearse any of the words on the list he wanted as many times as he wanted, while a tape recorder kept a record of what he said.

A typical example of a subject's rehearsal is shown in Figure 4.3. From the tape recordings, Rundus has computed the average number of times each word in the list was rehearsed, and from the free-recall he has computed the probability that each word was correctly recalled. The curve labeled ''Recall'' in Figure 4.4 shows the resulting function relating recall probability to number

Word presented	Words rehearsed
1. Reaction	reaction, reaction, reaction, reaction
2. Hoof	hoof, reaction, hoof, reaction
3. Blessing	blessing, hoof, reaction
4. Research	research, research, hoof, reaction
5. Candy	candy, hoof, reaction, reaction
6. Hardship	hardship, hoof, hardship, hoof
7. Kindness	kindness, candy, hardship, hoof
8. Nonsense	nonsense, kindness, candy, hardship
.	.
.	.
.	.

FIGURE 4.3   An example of some words presented in a list from Rundus' (1971) experiment along with a typical rehearsal protocol for the words.

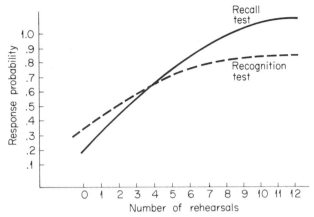

FIGURE 4.4   The more times a word is rehearsed, the higher the probability of its recall. (After Rundus *et al.*, 1970, Figure 2.)

of rehearsals. The results are clearcut: more rehearsal of a word leads to a greater probability of recalling that word.

Three weeks later, Rundus' subjects were asked to come back for a recognition test on the same words. As indicated by the "recognition test" curve in Figure 4.4, recognition as well as recall increased with more rehearsal.

Rundus continued: the primacy effect.   Not only has Rundus' work helped clarify how rehearsal may be involved in the transfer of information into long-term store, but it has also contributed to an understanding of the primacy portion of the free-recall curve. When discussing the serial position effect in Chapter 3, we have pointed out that the right-hand, or *recency*, part of the curve is a result of the high probability that the very recent items are in short-term store. We have so far given no explanation for the left-hand or primacy portion.

Rundus provides strong evidence that primacy may be a rehearsal effect. From Figure 4.3 we see that a subject usually rehearses three or four words at once. Notice now that when the first word of a list is presented to a subject, it is the only word that the subject has to worry about; therefore the word gets the subject's undivided attention and he rehearses it many times. The second word of the list, however, must share the subject's attention with the first word. Because the second word does not receive undivided attention, it is not rehearsed as much as the first word. When the third word is presented, it is rehearsed along with the first two words; it is therefore not rehearsed as much as either. This process is depicted by the protocol shown in Figure 4.3. To demonstrate the phenomenon somewhat more concretely, Rundus has plotted the recall probability and the number of rehearsals for a word as a function of the word's serial input position. This is shown in Figure 4.5. Notice that the

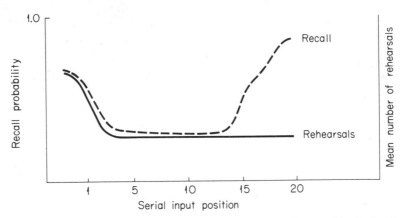

FIGURE 4.5   The mean number of rehearsals as a function of serial input position is given by the solid curve and should be read off the right-hand ordinate. Recall probability as a function of serial position is given by the dashed curve and should be read off the left-hand ordinate. Up until the recency portion, the two curves are extremely similar, suggesting that at least part of the explanation of the primacy effect is that the first few items in a list are rehearsed more. (After Rundus, 1971. Copyright 1971 by the American Psychological Association. Reproduced by permission.)

first few words in the list do indeed receive more rehearsals, and the rehearsal curve reflects the recall probability curve, up until the recency portion of the curve. Apparently, then, at least part of the explanation of the primacy effect is that the first few items in a list are rehearsed more than the other items.

The question now arose: was there anything *besides* the extra rehearsal that contributed to the primacy effect? To answer this question, Rundus compared performance on words at various serial positions that had received the same number of rehearsals. When this was done, the primacy effect disappeared! For example, words at Serial Position 1 that had received five rehearsals were recalled no better than words at Serial Position 7 that had received five rehearsals. The implication of this finding is that, in Rundus' study, words at the beginning of the list were recalled better *only* because they were rehearsed more.

Rehearsal is a handy construct for a theory of memory because it is a simple and a mathematically tractable entity to work with. Empirically we have seen a good deal of support for rehearsal as an information-transfer mechanism. In Rundus' experiments, for example, the concept of a rehearsal provides a powerful explanatory tool. However, in Rundus' experiments, subjects were *forced* to rehearse the words they were studying, and, in general, it is naive to think that rehearsal is the *only* means by which information is transferred to long-term store. Indeed when we introspect about how we learn things, we know that we do a good deal besides rehearsing. We elaborate on the information we are trying to remember; we form images; we use little mnemonic tricks; and we try to organize and integrate new information into the existing body of information that we already have stored. In the next two sections we discuss these "higher-level" transfer mechanisms.

MAINTENANCE REHEARSAL VERSUS ELABORATIVE REHEARSAL

Up until now, we have taken a somewhat simplistic view regarding the relationship between rehearsal and transfer of information to long-term store—namely, that rehearsal in any form always leads to transfer. Introspectively, however, this does not always seem to be the case. Sometimes, we have the experience of maintaining information in short-term store for a long time and then having no subsequent memory for it.

An important theoretical paper by Craik and Lockhart (1972) has suggested that there are at least two major types of rehearsal. The first type, called *maintenance rehearsal*, involves taking some kind of information and creating only a low-level, transient, acoustic code for it. This code may then be maintained indefinitely—but no information is transferred to long-term store. The second type of rehearsal is called *elaborative rehearsal*. Elaborative rehearsal involves taking information and creating elaborate codes—for example, associative codes, imaginal codes, organizational codes—that are stable and later retrievable from long-term store. We shall discuss two lines of evidence supporting this view.

Direct manipulation of maintenance time.   An experiment by Craik and Watkins (1973) provides what is probably the strongest evidence in favor of the maintenance–elaboration distinction. In this experiment, subjects were read long lists of words and were told that their only task was to report, at the end of the list, the last word in the list that began with some particular letter. Figure 4.6 provides an example of such a list. Here, the list is 24 words long, and the subject is told at the beginning that he will eventually be asked to report what is the last word in the list beginning with the letter "p" (hereafter referred to as a "P word"). Because the subject has no idea how many P words there will be in the list, he is forced to maintain in short-term store any given P word that occurs until it is replaced with another P word. This technique may be used to manipulate how long a subject maintains any given word in short-term store. In the example of Figure 4.5, the subject must maintain the word PEAR for a period of five intervening items until it gets replaced by POTATO. Likewise, POTATO is immediately replaced by PEN, which, in turn, is maintained through 12 intervening items until the end of the list. At that point the subject

Subject hears	Subject maintains	
1. Hat	—	
2. Class	—	
3. Hammer	—	
4. Glass	—	
5. Pear	*Pear*	First P word
6. Carrot	Pear	⎫
7. Frog	Pear	
8. England	Pear	⎬ 5 trials for Pear
9. Hat	Pear	
10. Wife	Pear	⎭
11. Potato	*Potato*	Second P word ⎫
12. Pen	*Pen*	Third P word ⎬ 0 trials for Potato
13. Horn	Pen	⎫
14. Love	Pen	
15. Smoke	Pen	
16. Leg	Pen	
17. Orange	Pen	
18. Coffee	Pen	⎬ 12 trials for Pen
19. Bed	Pen	
20. Night	Pen	
21. Ashtray	Pen	
22. Table	Pen	
23. Horse	Pen	
24. King	Pen	⎭

RECALL: Subject recalls "Pen"

FIGURE 4.6   An example of the sort of list used in the Craik and Watkins (1973) experiment.

will be asked to report the last P word in the list and will almost certainly correctly report PEN.

After several such lists are presented, an unexpected final free-recall test is given. Of interest is the function relating the final free-recall probability of a word to the length of time that word has been maintained in short-term store. Figure 4.7 shows this function: as can be seen, it is virtually flat. In terms of the Figure 4.6 example, PEN—which has been maintained in short-term store for a considerable length of time—is recalled no better than POTATO, which has been maintained only very briefly. The crucial point of this study is that rehearsal of information does not *automatically* lead to transfer of information to long-term store; it only leads to transfer when the subject *wants* to transfer it. The Craik and Watkins results provide very strong evidence for the notion that when purely maintenance rehearsal is being performed on some information, that information is not being copied to any extent into long-term store. (We shall, however, have an amendment to this conclusion in Chapter 5.)

Negative recency.   In an experiment by Craik (1970) subjects have been presented with a series of ten 15-word lists of words in a free-recall experiment. At the end of this series of lists, the subjects were given a final free-recall test for all 150 words. Figure 4.8 shows the result of this experiment, plotting the probability of a word being recalled in the final test as a

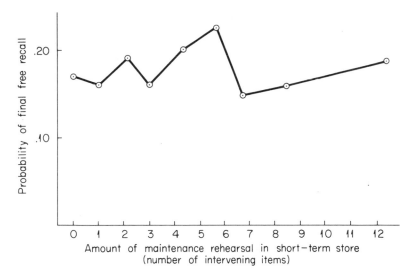

FIGURE 4.7   Results of the Craik and Watkins (1973) experiment: probability of final free-recall as a function of maintenance time. (Adapted from Craik & Watkins, 1973.)

function of the word's initial serial input position. Of interest is the fact that the last few words in the list were recalled somewhat more poorly than words from the middle of the list. Craik attributed this finding to the fact that the last few words in the list were probably rehearsed somewhat less than the words in the middle of the list (for example, the last word in the list would only be rehearsed for a very short period of time before the recall signal was given).

FIGURE 4.8   Results of the Craik (1970) study: probability of final free-recall as a function of original serial input position. (After Craik, 1970, Figure 2.)

A challenge to this interpretation was leveled by Watkins and Watkins (1974). Another interpretation, they pointed out, would go as follows: subjects in Craik's experiment knew when the end of the list was coming, and they knew that very shortly, they would be able to recall the last few words from short-term store. Therefore, there was no need to perform any elaborative rehearsal of these words. Instead, the words needed to be maintained only until the recall signal was given. In other words, this explanation attributes negative recency to the fact that the last few words in the list received only maintenance rehearsal, whereas the other words (which subjects knew they would have to recall from long-term store) received elaborative rehearsal.

To distinguish between these two explanations, Watkins and Watkins performed a free-recall experiment using lists of varying lengths. In one condition, a subject knew how long the list was and furthermore was informed when the end of the list was near. In the second condition, the subject had no idea how long the list was; the end of the list (and the recall signal) therefore came as a surprise. Again, after completion of all lists, an unexpected final free-recall test was given. According to a straight rehearsal explanation (Craik's explanation) the two conditions should both have produced negative recency in final free recall because in both cases the last few words received fewer rehearsals. The maintenance–elaboration explanation, however, would predict negative recency only in the condition where the subject knew when the end of the list was coming, for if he did not know this, he would continue giving words elaborative rehearsal right up until the time that the experimenter popped up with a recall command. The results left no room for doubt: the negative recency finding was nicely replicated when subjects knew the list length; when they did not know, however, negative recency disappeared.

The experiments by Craik and Watkins and by Watkins and Watkins therefore provide fairly convincing evidence that purely maintenance rehearsal does not act as a mechanism for information transfer. What about the other side of the coin, elaborative rehearsal? Much of what modern theorists call elaborative rehearsal has been studied for years under the general label of *organization*.

ORGANIZATION

When we learn a new thoerem in mathematics or read a novel in an English course, we typically try to organize the material. Organization can mean either (1) trying to make it fit into some preexisting logical framework or (2) trying to create some new logical framework that binds the material into some cohesive unit.

Organization and mnemonics. A *mnemonic* is a technique (often referred to as a "memory trick") for organizing information so that it can be more easily remembered. Mnemonic devices have been around since the time of the ancient Greeks; the Greek poet Simonides, for one, used them to remember all sorts of things. The most famous story about Simonides was told by Cicero in *De Oratore*. One night, Simonides had just finished reciting poetry at a huge banquet when he was abruptly called away from the banquet hall by a messenger. Moments later, the entire roof of the hall caved in completely, crushing the guests beneath the ruins, and so mutilating them that not one could be identified. The grief-striken relatives of these unfortunate guests were anxious to find the bodies of their loved ones so that they could be properly buried. At first glance this task seemed impossible, but, to the amazement of all, Simonides reported that he was able to remember the exact place where each guest had been sitting, and thus was able to identify the bodies. Simonides learned something very important from this tragic experience. He could use his location technique to remember all sorts of objects and ideas; he simply assigned them fixed positions in space.

This particular mnemonic technique has come to be called the "method of loci." To use the method of loci, suppose that you have to give a speech from memory. First, you imagine a place that you are familiar with, such as your house. Now, you mentally "put" various parts of the speech in various parts of the house. The initial joke, for example, might be placed in the front hall, the first point of the introduction in the sitting room, and so on. At the time you have to give the speech you then merely take a mental "walk" through the house retrieving each of the points of the speech in sequence. It sounds very strange, but it is a technique that works well for most people.

In general, mnemonics may be used to help us learn faster and recall better. When we had to learn the number of days in each month, we learned "Thirty days hath September, April, June, and November . . ." When we were learning the proper ordering of the letters *i* and *e* in spelling English words, we learned the phrase, "*i* before *e* except after *c*." Some of us learned the spelling of "arithmetic" by remembering "a rat in the house may eat the ice cream." And to remember the order of the avenues Lexington, Park, and Madison in New York City, one of the authors relied on the phrase "Ladies Prefer Men (when traveling west)." Mnemonic devices are exceedingly useful.

A scientist, however, wants more than anecdotes and stories about Greek poets to be certain about the power of mnemonics. Recently, therefore, rigorous laboratory experiments have been conducted on the topic. In this section, we shall discuss some of these experiments.

Narrative chaining—a powerful mnemonic. Bower and Clark (1969) gave students lists of ten unrelated words in a *serial learning* task (in a serial learning task the words have to be remembered in the exact order in which they are presented). Half the students learned the words by making up and weaving a story around the words. If the words "table, light, ashtray, frog . . ." began the list, a student's story might begin "There was a *table* in the kitchen that had a *light* on it. It also had an *ashtray*. There was a *frog* jumping back and forth between the light and ashtray . . .'' The other half of the students in the experiment were given the words and simply told to memorize them for recall. Both groups of students could recall the list almost perfectly when tested immediately after the list was studied. (It is not hard to do this when the list consists of only ten words.) The same procedure was then repeated again and again until a total of 12 lists of words had been learned. After the twelfth list, students were unexpectedly given the first word of the first list and were asked to recall the remaining words in the list. This procedure was repeated for the rest of the lists. At this point there was an emormous difference between the two groups of subjects: those who had made up stories recalled an average of 93% of the words, whereas those in the control (nonstory) group recalled an average of only 13% of the words. This simple technique of narrative chaining therefore increased retention by a factor of almost seven.

Imagery.   In addition to the narrative chaining method, Bower (1973) has also found improved recall with imagery techniques. Imagery may be studied in a paired-associate paradigm in which subjects learn such noun pairs as DOG–CIGAR. Later, at the time of the test, the left-hand word is presented as a cue and the subject must recall the right-hand word. In Bower's experiments, some subjects were instructed to learn the pairs by imagining a visual scene or mental picture in which these two objects are interacting in some way. For example, when presented with DOG–CIGAR, the subject may have conjured up a mental image of a dog smoking a big black cigar. Subjects given imagery instructions performed almost twice as well as control subjects, who were simply told to rehearse the pairs over and over.

Organization and the Hebb paradigm.   Using a paradigm quite similar to the one developed by Hebb, Bower gathered additional evidence for the power of organization (Bower, 1970; Bower & Winzenz, 1969). Bower presented 12-digit number strings, such as 828271182890, which were read aloud to the subject. The string just given might be read as "eighty-two, eight twenty-seven, one thousand one hundred-eighty-two, eight ninety." Recall performance on these repeated strings improved over trials, replicating Hebb's original result. Bower's innovation, however, was to keep the same sequence of digits for some of the strings but to change the verbal grouping. For example, the above string might be read as "eight, twenty-eight, two seventy-one . . ." the second time it was presented, and "eight twenty-eight, two, seventy-one . . ." the third time. When the sequence stayed the same but the organization was changed, recall did not improve at all, supporting the notion that organization of the digits can strongly influence memory performance.

Organization in free recall.   A great deal of the empirical work in the area of organization has been done using a free-recall paradigm. Bousfield's

(1953) study is an example. Bousfield presented his subjects with a 60-word list composed of 15 instances of each of four conceptual categories: animals, names, professions, and vegetables. The 60 words in the list were presented in a random order rather than by categories. Bousfield observed that when his subjects attempted to recall the 60-word list, words belonging to the same category tended to cluster together. For example, a subject who was presented with a list beginning "horse, George, teacher, lamb, doctor, Sylvia . . ." may have begun his recall with "horse, lamb"; "George, Sylvia"; "teacher, doctor . . .". This "category clustering" effect is even stronger when all items from one category are presented contiguously (Cofer, Bruce, & Reicher, 1966; Puff, 1966). When recall of a list composed of items from several categories is compared to recall of a list of unrelated words, the former is far superior. If the material to be learned has some organization to it, recall is better and clustering tends to occur. Subjects appear to be able to take advantage of the structure in the material they are learning.

There are two possible reasons for this: (1) the organized material is easier to store in long-term store or (2) the organized material is easier to retrieve from long-term store. An experiment by Tulving and Pearlstone (1966) bears on this point. In Tulving and Pearlstone's experiment, two groups of subjects learned a long list constructed from instances of natural categories. Because the two groups learned their lists under identical conditions, they should have stored them equally well. Later, one group of subjects was given the category names as recall cues, whereas the other group was given no cues. For a 48-item list composed of 12 categories with four members each, the "category cue" subjects recalled words from 11.5 categories, whereas the subjects who were not given cues recalled words from only 7.3 categories on the average. In terms of the number of items recalled within a category there was no difference between the two groups of subjects; both groups recalled 2.6 items per category. The fact that the group given the category cues recalled many more words suggests that in this experiment the cues did indeed facilitate retrieval rather than storage.

Subjective organization.   The work of Bousfield and others has shown that if the material a person is learning is organized in some way, the person can use this organization to his benefit. If the words in a list fall into natural categories, we observe clustering in the recall of those words. What happens in the situation in which the experimenter does not use a categorized word list but uses a list of apparently unrelated words? For example, suppose a subject is asked to memorize a list beginning with these items: "hat, picture, lamb, grandfather. . . ." No two items seem to fall easily into a single conceptual category. In an experiment by Endel Tulving (1962), 16 unrelated words were presented to a subject one at a time and the subject tried to recall the words in any order he wished. The subject then studied the list again, recalled again,

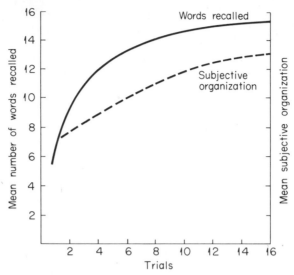

FIGURE 4.9   Both number of words recalled and subjective organization in a multitrial free-recall experiment increase over trials. (After Tulving, 1962. Copyright 1962 by the American Psychological Association. Reproduced by permission.)

studied, recalled, and so on, for several trials (a paradigm called *multitrial free recall*). As you might expect, further trials led to better recall, as shown in Figure 4.9. After the subject had studied the list once, he recalled only about six of the words; after 16 presentations of the list, however, he recalled 15 of the words. Of interest in this experiment was that subjects tended to recall words in the same order on successive trials. To do this, subjects were using a strategy that Tulving termed "subjective organization." For example, a subject might recall the words "picture" and "grandfather" contiguously trial after trial. Further trials led to more subjective organization, or an even greater tendency to recall words in the same order from one trial to the next. This phenomenon is also depicted in Figure 4.9.

Both Mandler (1967) and Tulving (1968) have argued that the observed improvement in recall is caused by the increasing subjective organization. What happens is that subjects set up groupings of words in the list. For example, a subject may group "picture" and "grandfather" together because he has seen many pictures of his own or other people's grandfathers. As the experiment progresses, more and more words are added to the basic groupings. For example, "hat" may be added because the subject's grandfather usually wore a hat when having his picture taken. At recall time, a subject first retrieves a grouping and then reports the words in that grouping.

The phenomenon of subjective organization is therefore similar to the organization we observed in categorized word lists, where subjects could use the category name (either by recalling it or by hearing it from the experimenter) to retrieve the items in that category. What is important in both the experiments on category clustering and the experiments on subjective organization is the fact that certain words are consistently recalled together, even though they were not necessarily presented together. Such consistencies highlight the importance of organization in recall.

Organization and retrieval.   There is a frequently used example demonstrating that if we are asked to retrieve information in the way in which it is organized, our job is very easy; if asked to retrieve it in some other way, our job becomes much harder. The instruction to "name the 12 months of the year in chronological order" is easy for most of us; but "name the 12 months of the year arranged alphabetically" generally yields "uh . . . uh . . . April . . . August . . . uh . . . December." In their natural order, the months of the year form a very familiar organized series of words; in any other order they do not.

Chunks revisited.   So far, we have discussed various phenomena falling under the general classification of "organization." These phenomena have included mnemonic tricks, such as narrative chaining and imagery, along with category clustering, and subjective organization. A possible unifying factor underlying all these different types of organization is the concept of chunks.

Remember what a chunk is—it is anything that is stored in some unitary way in long-term store, such as a digit, a letter, a word, or a proverb. Basically, the process of organization can be thought of as the act of taking many little chunks and welding them into fewer larger chunks. For example, in a paired-associate experiment using imagery, two separate chunks, say the words "piano" and "cigar," are welded into one chunk—the image. In a narrative chaining experiment, a series of unrelated chunks—words—are welded into one chunk—the story. Likewise, the phenomenon of category clustering consists basically of taking words and welding them into a chunk organized around the category. Subjective organization consists of doing the same thing, in a somewhat more idiosyncratic way; the three unrelated words, "grandfather," "picture," and "hat" become welded into one chunk involving a picture of your grandfather wearing a hat. As we saw in the example of retrieving the months of the year, retrieving information is much easier when that information is all organized into one chunk (the months in chronological order) than when it is organized into many chunks (the months in alphabetical order).

Organization and rehearsal.   Because we have seen that organization is so important and pervasive in everyday life, you may wonder what the importance of rehearsal is and why we spent so much time discussing rehearsal. The answer lies in the fact that, from a theoretical standpoint, rehearsal and organization are two different levels of behavior, with rehearsal being a lower, more basic level. To make this notion clearer, an analogy to chemistry may be appropriate. Chemists study both basic units (such as atoms) and larger units (molecules). An understanding of both these lower level and higher level units is necessary in order to understand the structure of matter. Rehearsal may be thought of as analogous to atoms, whereas organization may be thought of as analogous to molecules; an understanding of both these lower level and higher level processes is necessary for understanding the structure of memory.

TYPE OF INFORMATION IN LONG-TERM STORE

When discussing the nature of information stored in short-term store, we presented evidence that it was acoustic in form. If a subject made an error when trying to report what he saw or heard in a short-term memory experiment, the errors usually sounded like the correct item. If long-term store were really different from short-term store then it would be reasonable to expect different types of information to be found in the two types of memory stores.

Semantic information. A number of experiments have suggested that the information in long-term store is basically *semantic*, that is, information relating to *meaning*. The studies, like the short-term memory studies, have examined the kinds of errors that are made. Suppose a subject is in a memory experiment that has a long retention interval as part of the procedure. If the subject sees the word CAR, he is much more likely later on to erroneously think he saw the word AUTO, VEHICLE, TRIUMPH, or BUICK, which are semantically related to CAR, than to think he saw TAR or CAP, which sound like CAR but are not related in meaning. These studies, which are sometimes referred to as *false recognition experiments*, strongly suggest that the dominant mode of representation in long-term store is semantic (Anisfeld & Knapp, 1968; Baddeley, 1966; Grossman & Eagle, 1970).

The same conclusion was reached by Kintsch and Buschke (1969) using a somewhat different procedure. Kintsch and Buschke took advantage of the fact that the degree of similarity of words in a list powerfully influences the ease or speed with which a subject can learn to give the words in order. A list with a good deal of similarity, such as "car, auto, vehicle, Triumph, and Buick," would be hard to give in order; it would be hard to remember which word went in which position.

Kintsch and Buschke's experiment was based on the following reasoning: if long-term store involves semantic encoding and short-term store does not, then two semantically related words, such as CAR and AUTO, should interfere with each other only when a recall test occurs after a long retention interval, for it is only then that the items are retrieved from long-term store. If CAR and AUTO are presented early in a list of words to be remembered, therefore, a subject should have difficulty. If CAR and AUTO appear late in the list (that is, just before the recall test when they are in short-term store) a subject should have relatively less difficulty.

On the other side of the coin, short-term store supposedly involves acoustic encoding and long-term store supposedly does not. Therefore, two acoustically related words, such as CAR and TAR, should interfere with each other when a recall test occurs soon after the words are presented. If CAR and TAR are presented late in a list of words to be remembered, a subject should therefore have difficulty, whereas CAR and TAR presented early in the list should not cause much trouble.

In one of Kintsch and Buschke's experiments, subjects were presented lists of 16 words. After the 16 words were presented, one of the words was repeated and the subject had to respond with the word that had originally followed the repeated word. There were two types of lists: one type consisted of eight pairs of synonyms (CAR and AUTO) presented in a random order, and the other type consisted of 16 unrelated words. Figure 4.10a shows the probability of correctly recalling words from various positions for both types of lists. As expected, semantically related words cause difficulty only when presented early in a list.

In a second experiment, Kintsch and Buschke exchanged the synonym pairs for pairs of words that were acoustically related. The results (Figure 4.10b) show that acoustically related words interfere with each other when recently presented but not when presented early in a list.

Acoustic savings in long-term store.   Although the preceding discussion has focussed on semantic information in long-term store, it runs counter to common sense that semantic information is the *only* kind of information in long-term store. Consider, for example, a question, raised by Posner (1967): if

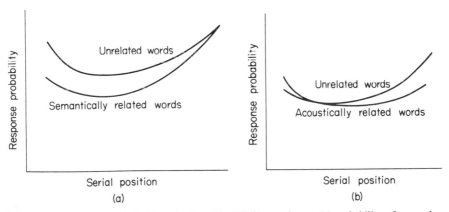

FIGURE 4.10   Results of the Kintsch – Buschke (1969) experiment: (a) probability of correctly recalling words at various serial positions for unrelated vs semantically similar words; (b) probability of correctly recalling words at various serial positions for unrelated versus acoustically similar words. (After Kintsch & Buschke, 1969, Figures 1 and 3, respectively. Copyright 1969 by the American Psychological Association. Reproduced by permission.)

semantic information is the only kind of information in long-term store, how do we ever learn to recognize other accents? How are we ever able to tell that one person is speaking English with a southern accent whereas another has a French accent? How do we know a man's voice from a woman's, for that matter? A recent study by Nelson and Rothbart (1972) provides direct evidence that acoustic as well as semantic information is stored in long-term store. Nelson and Rothbart's basic procedure was to present information for a subject to memorize and then to give the subject some time to forget some of the information. The important question is: of the information *remaining* in long-term store, is any of the information acoustic?

Specifically, Nelson and Rothbart presented subjects with a paired-associate task; subjects learned number–word pairs, such as "37–doe" or "29–cat," well enough to be able to produce the response (the word) when given the stimulus (the number). When all of the pairs were learned (in long-term store) the subject left, went about his normal activities, and returned to the laboratory four weeks later. At this point, each stimulus was presented and the subject tried to remember the response that went with it. As would be expected, many of the responses had been forgotten. If a response had been forgotten, the stimulus that went with it was *re-paired* with a new response. For example, if "doe" was not remembered as the response to "37," then 37 was re-paired with a new response. The new response bore one of three relationships to the old response: (1) it was identical to the old response (37–doe), (2) it was acoustically similar to the old response (37–dough), or (3) it was unrelated to the old response (37–peach). Now the subject had to relearn all the new pairings. Which type of new pairing should be easiest to relearn?

Almost 100 years ago, Ebbinghaus (1885) showed that the relearning of an old response is easier than the learning of a new response; this is called the *savings effect*. Therefore, of the three re-pairings listed above, "37–doe" was easiest to relearn. This finding simply indicates that there is *some* information left in forgotten pairings. What about the other types of re-pairings? If there is no acoustic information about the original response left in long-term store, then the acoustically similar response should be as difficult to relearn as the unrelated response. If there is some acoustic information remaining, however, then the acoustically similar response should be easier to relearn.

The results are shown in Figure 4.11. When the new response was acoustically similar to the old one, it was much easier to relearn. We can therefore conclude that at least part of the information stored in long-term store is acoustic.

What is stored: A summary. A popular view about what is stored—that only acoustic information is in short-term store whereas only semantic information is in long-term store—has received support from experiments showing that the confusion errors in short-term store tend to be acoustic in nature, whereas those in long-term store tend to be semantic in nature.

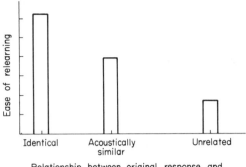

FIGURE 4.11   Ease of relearning the three types of new responses. Relearning was easiest when the new response was identical to the old one. When the new response was acoustically similar, relearning was easier than when it was unrelated to the old response. (Adapted from Nelson & Rothbart, 1972. Copyright 1972 by the American Psychological Association. Reproduced by permission.)

Although experiments have been published that do not find evidence for acoustic information in long-term store (Kintsch & Buschke, 1969, for one) the more recent work of Nelson and Rothbart (1972) and other researchers (Baddeley, 1970; Buschke & Lenon, 1969; Laurence, 1970; Wickens, Ory, & Graf, 1970) reveals that retrieval from long-term store may also involve use of acoustic information. It is likely that the Kintsch and Buschke procedure was simply not sensitive enough to reveal the existence of acoustic information in long-term store. In any event, the popular view is in need of revision. A potentially more viable view has been suggested by Nelson (in 1970; reported by Smith, Barresi, & Gross, 1971): both acoustic and semantic information are stored in both short-term store and long-term store; however, the short-term retrieval process is primarily sensitive to acoustic information, whereas the long-term retrieval process is primarily sensitive to semantic information. In Chapter 6 we reopen the topic of what is stored in long-term store when we consider some experiments using more complex materials.

FORGETTING FROM LONG-TERM STORE

"The horror of that moment," the King went on, "I shall never, never, never forget!"

"You will, though," the Queen said, "if you don't make a memorandum of it."

Lewis Carroll

She was speaking for most of us when an anonymous little girl proclaimed: "My memory is the thing I forget with." Most of us experience forgetting all

FIGURE 4.12   "The Thinker" is the name of Rodin's famous sculpture representing a man searching his mind. Add a wrinkled brow and a slightly anguished facial expression and we have "The Forgetter"—he knows the fact he is searching for is there but he just cannot find it.

the time: we grope futilely for a name to go with that face we see again at a party, for the punchline of a joke we heard someone tell just the day before, or for the answer to an exam question that we studied for and knew only yesterday. Forgetting is so common that by now it would be a very easy word to elicit from your partner in a game of charades (see Figure 4.12). Simply get in a position resembling that taken by Rodin's "The Thinker," wrinkle your brow, look slightly anguished, and lo and behold you have "The Forgetter" (Underwood, 1964).

Interference theory.   One of the oldest and most widely held explanations of forgetting is that people forget an event because something else they have learned prevents the event from being remembered. One event blocks or interferes with another. Interference theorists say that "interference" is going on in this situation: "Who won the ball game yesterday?" "Uh . . . uh . . . uh . . . I keep wanting to say the Red Sox, but I know that's not right."

One of the oldest studies of interference was one in which students learned lists of nonsense syllables and immediately afterwards they either (1) went to sleep or (2) carried on their normal activities (Jenkins & Dallenbach, 1924). At the end of 1, 2, 4, and 8 hours, the students were asked to recall the material they had learned. Of course, the subjects in the sleeping condition had to be awakened after each of these intervals on four different nights. Figure 4.13 shows the forgetting curves following sleep and waking conditions. Several results are clear: for all retention intervals, recall was better after sleep than after being awake. After 8 hours of being awake only about one nonsense syllable could be recalled, whereas after the same amount of sleep almost six

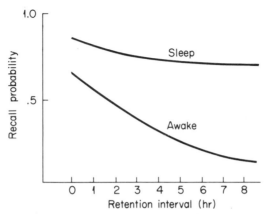

FIGURE 4.13   Amount of material remembered after sleep and waking conditions. When subjects sleep after learning some new material their retention is superior. (After Jenkins & Dallenbach, 1924.

times as many syllables were recalled. In an extension of these results, a more recent sleep study showed that retention during sleep while dreaming is inferior to retention during sleep without dreams (Yaroush, Sullivan, & Ekstrand, 1971).

Two types of events may have potentially interfered with the retention of the nonsense syllables: events that have happened before the nonsense syllables are learned and events that happen afterward. The interference theory of forgetting really consists of two subtheories. The first one deals with the fact that earlier learning interferes with our ability to recall newly learned material, a phenomenon called *proactive interference*. The other subtheory deals with the fact that new learning interferes with our ability to recall previously learned material, a phenomenon called *retroactive interference*. Figure 4.14 illustrates these two types of interference.

Retroactive interference.   Retroactive interference (or retroactive inhibition) refers to the fact that something learned during a retention interval

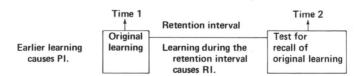

FIGURE 4.14   Interference theory. At Time 1, some material is learned. After a retention interval, the material is tested for recall at Time 2. Other material learned before Time 1 produces proactive interference (PI), whereas other learning occuring during the retention interval produces retroactive interference (RI).

produces forgetting of previously learned material. Here is the basic paradigm for a typical retroactive interference experiment:

EXPERIMENTAL GROUP	LEARNS INFORMATION A	LEARNS INFORMATION B	RECALLS INFORMATION A
CONTROL GROUP	LEARNS INFORMATION A	NO NEW LEARNING	RECALLS INFORMATION A

The experimental group learns and then recalls Information A, but between learning and recall new information (B) is learned. The control group learns and recalls Information A, with no new learning in between. As may be expected from interference theory, the experimental group tends to have much more difficulty recalling the original Information A. Furthermore, the harder Information B is to learn, the greater the interference. It therefore appears that learning Information B acts to disrupt or interfere somehow with the current retention of Information A.

Proactive interference.   Proactive interference (or proactive inhibition) refers to the fact that something learned prior to new material produces forgetting of that new material. Old habits interfere with the acquisition of new ones. Here is the basic paradigm for a typical proactive interference experiment:

EXPERIMENTAL GROUP	LEARNS INFORMATION B	LEARNS INFORMATION A	RECALLS INFORMATION A
CONTROL GROUP	NO PRIOR LEARNING	LEARNS INFORMATION A	RECALLS INFORMATION A

The experimental group learns Information B before learning and then learns and retrieves Information A. The control group simply learns and retrieves Information A with no prior learning. The control group then has an easier time recalling Task A than does the experimental group.

Retroactive interference is a somewhat "intuitive" phenomenon in the sense that we are all aware that the more time we wait after learning something, the more likely it is that we will have forgotten it. Proactive interference, in contrast, was less obvious and it was not really studied systematically until a psychologist named Benton Underwood observed a strange phenomenon (Underwood, 1948a, b, 1949). Underwood noted that when a typical subject in his laboratory learned a list of nonsense syllables perfectly and then was tested 24 hours later, he had forgotten only about 20% of the items. However, Ebbinghaus, the great master at recalling nonsense syllables, forgot about 65% of the material he had learned. Was it possible that a college student who had learned only one list could remember nonsense syllables better than Ebbinghaus, who had studied hundreds and hundreds of lists?

Reflecting on the mystery, Underwood noticed that most of his subjects had been college students who had learned few or no paired-associate lists prior to entering his laboratory. Conversely, Ebbinghaus's learning of any given list was preceded by learning of many prior lists. Underwood formulated the hypothesis that memory performance is made worse the more prior lists that a subject has learned. Underwood then tested his hypothesis, reporting:

> . . . we give the subject a second list to learn and test him on this list 24 hours later. This time his performance is not quite so good as it was in [the first list]; he forgets more than 20 percent. We go on in the same way with a third list, a fourth, a fifth and so on up to 20 lists. Plotting his successive performances on a graph, we find a startlingly sharp rise in his rate of forgetting. . . . In the case of the 20th list, 24 hours after learning it he has forgotten 80 percent of the items [Underwood, 1964, p. 5].

The experiment shows how a college student can forget only 20% whereas Ebbinghaus forgot 65%. Twenty percent represents the amount of forgetting of the first list. The more lists a subject learns, the more he forgets of the last list he has studied. It is a wonder that Ebbinghaus, with all his studying, forgot *only* 65%. Forgetting appears to be strongly influenced by the activities a subject has engaged in before a recall test.

Theoretical basis for interference theory.   The mechanisms by which retroactive and proactive interference are thought to operate have their roots in the classical conditioning work of Pavlov (1927). As is fairly common knowledge, Pavlov used a paradigm in which he paired a *conditioned stimulus* (for example, a bell) with an *unconditioned stimulus* (for example, food). After a series of such pairings, the conditioned stimulus came to elicit the *conditioned response* of salivation.

Suppose now the conditioned stimulus (bell) continues to be presented but it is not paired with the unconditioned stimulus (food). The emission of the conditioned response gradually decreases, a phenomenon called *extinction*. The more the conditioned stimulus is presented in the absence of the unconditioned stimulus, the more extinction occurs. Finally, suppose a response is extinguished and a period of time is allowed to go by, and then the conditioned stimulus is presented again: lo and behold, the conditioned response occurs again. The longer the interval between the last extinction trial and the new presentation of the conditioned stimulus, the stronger is the conditioned response. This is known as *spontaneous recovery*.

With this background, we are ready to discuss the extinction or unlearning explanation of retroactive and proactive interference. Consider first a three-stage retroactive interference experiment:

1. Subject learns a paired associate list with "A" stimuli and "B" responses (referred to as List A–B).
2. Subject learns a second paired-associate list with the "A" stimuli re-paired with new "C" responses (List A–C).
3. Subject must recall the "B" responses in the presence of "A" stimuli.

As discussed above, a subject's performance in Stage 3 is likely to be considerably poorer than that of a control subject who has not had the A–B interpolated learning. Furthermore, the more A–C learning there is, the poorer is the final A–B performance. Note that this is completely explicable within a Pavlovian framework. The A–B list corresponds to the original conditioning. During A–C learning, the original B responses to the A stimuli become extinguished, because they are elicited but not reinforced.

Consider now a proactive interference experiment. Using the same notation, the subject goes through the following stages:

1. Subject learns List A–B.
2. Subject learns List A–C.
3. After some retention interval, subject recalls List A–C.

Again, as already discussed, the subjects' final (Stage 3) performance on List A–C is likely to be worse than that of a control subject who has not learned the original List A–B. Furthermore, as the retention interval between stages two and three increases, final A–C performance becomes progressively worse; in fact, subjects trying to remember the C responses emit increasing numbers of the original B responses with increasing retention interval (Briggs, 1954). Again, this result fits very neatly into the Pavlovian framework, which assumes that over the retention interval the original A–B responses are undergoing spontaneous recovery and therefore become progressively more likely to interfere.

FORGETTING AS RETRIEVAL FAILURE

Interference theory, which has its roots in stimulus–response psychology, is one framework for viewing the phenomenon of forgetting. A different framework, which is more in line with the information-processing approach, views forgetting not in terms of unlearning or competition of conditioned responses, but as a failure to retrieve some desired information. Just about all of us have experienced the following event: we are desperately trying to think of some piece of information but, hard as we try, we cannot get it. Then, sometime later, when conditions are different, that piece of information seems to come back practically spontaneously. Forgetting has been only temporary. Because this happens so often, many psychologists have argued that forgetting is much like being unable to find something that we have misplaced somewhere. Forgetting occurs because the information we seek is temporarily inaccessible; if only we had the right retrieval cue, the information we seek could be successfully retrieved.

Before we can discuss experiments that support the retrieval failure idea, we need to consider some basic questions about how searches through memory may be conducted: are they sequential or do we somehow "directly contact" the information we want?

Ways of searching long-term store.   Suppose someone asks you for the capital of California. If you must search through all the information in your memory sequentially, it would take forever to come up with the answer. Sylvan Tomkins (1970) has argued that if you had to answer the simple question "What is your name?" a sequential search of long-term store may take you over 400 years before you find the answer. Norman (1968) similarily points out that if we have stored N items in memory, a sequential search takes approximately $N/2$ attempts to find any specific item. With such a large system as long-term store, such a search strategy is obviously impractical.

Alternatively, the retrieval system may contact only those locations indicated in the question asked of it. In the present example, the system might make direct contact with "California" and with "state capitals." After direct contact takes place, the system then searches this information in more detail. This notion of a direct contact search scheme is favored by many psychologists. The search is thought to be "limited" in the sense that we do not continue searching forever. We have "stop rules" that tell us when to give up the search. For example, we may try to think of the capital of California for 1 minute, and then give up if we cannot think of it. A "direct contact–limited search" mechanism is quite reasonable; for one thing, it predicts that our ability to find an item we are looking for depends on how large the set is in which we are searching. If the search set is very large, the stop rule is likely to be applied before we find the item we are looking for.

Reducing the search set.   In 1968 Ronald Hopkins and Richard Atkinson did a two-stage experiment; in the first stage, subjects studied a list of 75 proper names of well-known people (such as Richard Burton) and then tried to write down as many of the names as they could remember. The next day, the subjects were shown a series of 150 pictures, one at a time; their job was to name the person in the picture. Seventy-five of the 150 pictures corresponded to names that had been on the previous day's list. For half of the trials, the subject was "informed" as to whether he had or had not studied the name the day before. The experiment therefore had four different conditions. The mean proportion of times the subject correctly reported the name in each of the four conditions is shown in Table 4.1.

Notice that subjects did much better on pictures of people whose names they had studied than on pictures of people whose names they had not studied. Because the set of all studied names is a much smaller set than the set of all names of famous people, it is no surprise that the subject did better on studied names. However, the difference between studied and nonstudied is not the most interesting finding in this experiment. If there really is some loss in long-term store then the nonstudied pictures may have been worse off because

TABLE 4.1

Mean Proportion of Times that the Correct Response
was Given in the Hopkins and Atkinson (1968) Experiment[a]

	Studied	Not studied
Informed	.46	.26
Not Informed	.40	.26

[a] Adapted from Hopkins and Atkinson (1968).

they have had more time to suffer the loss. The interesting difference in this experiment is between the informed and noninformed conditions for subjects who had studied the names (.46 versus .40). Because this information was given at the time the subject was attempting to recall the name, the differences in performance cannot be attributed to differences in the way the two types of pictures had been stored. The recall differences for informed versus noninformed must be because the informed condition has provided an additional retrieval cue.

Retrieval cues. An experiment by Endel Tulving and Zena Pearlstone (1966), discussed above, demonstrates the power of providing the proper retrieval cue. Subjects in this experiment were given a list consisting of category names (such as animal, fruit, crime) and, following each category name, one or more instances of that category (for example, for the categories just mentioned, typical instances might be horse, plum, and murder). The subjects were asked to memorize only the instances but not the names of the categories themselves.

Later on, subjects were asked to write down as many of the words as they could remember on a sheet of paper. Half of the subjects had a blank sheet and the remaining subjects had a sheet that contained all the category names. Who recalled the most instances? The subjects who had been given the category names as cues recall more instances, as can be seen in Figure 4.15.

Consider what happened in the condition when subjects were given a list of 48 items (12 categories of four words each). The subjects who were given the category names recalled about 30 words, whereas those who were given no cues recalled about 20 words, on the average. Later on, when the latter group of subjects were provided with the category names, they could recall about 28 words from the list. Where did those extra eight items come from? They must have been stored in the subject's memory somewhere, but a retrieval cue was needed before they could be found. This experiment clearly shows a case in which supposedly lost information has been recovered. Providing the proper retrieval cue is one of the best ways to facilitate recall.

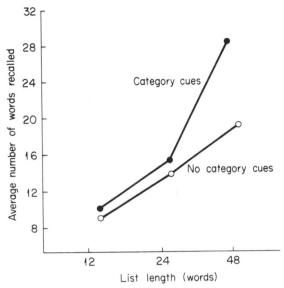

FIGURE 4.15 Average number of words recalled as a function of list length in the Tulving – Pearlstone (1966) experiment. More words were recalled when category cues are provided (●) than when they were not (○).

Later work (Tulving & Thomson, 1973) reveals an even more striking example of the power of a retrieval cue: under certain conditions a subject can completely fail to recognize a word he has learned, yet he can immediately recall that word when provided with the right retrieval cue. Consider the experiment (see Figure 4.16). The subject saw a list of word pairs: the cue word on the left is in lower case and the word to be remembered on the right is in capital letters (for example, pretty–BLUE; country–OPEN; fruit–FLOWER). The subject's task was to remember the capital-lettered words only. After the words were learned, the subject took a free association test in which he was given a different list of stimulus words, and he had to write down a number of words that he thought of as associated with the stimulus words. The subject was allowed, if he wished, to include in the free association any of the words he had previously memorized or any of the cue words. For example, if the subject had been given the italicized words on the left as stimuli, he might have responded with the words on the right:

lake   boat, fish, swim, water, cold, blue, breeze
eat   food, fruit, flower, picnic, lunch, dinner, fish
night day, sky, open, black

After finishing the free association test, the subject circled those words in his free association that he recognized as being on the list of previously memorized

Stage 1:	Cue words	To-be-remembered words		
A subject learns a list of paired words and must remember the words on the right	whistle	BALL		
	pretty	BLUE		
	noise	WIND		
	fruit	FLOWER		
	country	OPEN		
		etc.		

Stage 2:				
The subject is shown a list of words and is asked to free associate to those words; after free association the subject circles any words that he remembers as being on the list he originally learned	lake:	boat	cool	(blue)
	eat:	food	fruit	(flower)
	fast:	car	woman	race
	soft:	down	bed	skin
	clean:	bath	living	soap
	night:	day	open	sky
			etc.	

Stage 3:		
The subject is given the cue words from the original list and must write down the corresponding to-be-remembered words	country	_open_
	fruit	_____
	bath	_____
	noise	_____
		etc.

FIGURE 4.16   A three stage experiment by Tulving and Thomson (1971).

words. About 25% of these previously memorized words were recognized. At this point in the experiment, the subject was given a final recall test in which he was shown the cue words from the original list and tried to recall the words to be remembered. Now, the average subject recalled over 60% of the memorized words; his recall obviously included many of the words that he had failed to recognize just a few minutes earlier. Once again, retrieval cues really do help; in this case one particular word (the cue word) may be a more effective retrieval cue for a word to be remembered than having the entire word spelled out on a sheet of paper.

Repression as retrieval failure.   Memories that may cause us great unhappiness if they were brought to mind often appear to be "forgotten." However, are they really lost from memory or are they simply temporarily repressed as originally suggested by Freud (1922)? *Repression* is the phenomenon that prevents someone from remembering an event that can cause him pain and suffering. One way that we know that these memories are repressed and not completely lost is that the methods of free association and hypnosis and other special techniques used by psychotherapists can be used to bring repressed material to mind and can help a person remember things that he has failed to remember earlier.

A laboratory analogy to repression can be found in an experiment by A. F. Zeller (1950). Zeller arranged a situation so that one group of students underwent an unhappy "failure" experience right after they had successfully learned a list of nonsense syllables. When tested later, these subjects showed much poorer recall of the nonsense syllables compared to a control group, who had not experienced failure. When this same "failure" group was later allowed to succeed on the same task that they had earlier failed, their recall showed tremendous improvement. This experiment indicates that when the reason for the repression is removed, when material to be remembered is no longer associated with negative effects, a person no longer experiences retrieval failure.

RETRIEVAL FAILURE VERSUS INTERFERENCE THEORY: ONE POSSIBLE TEST

In 1970, Richard Shiffrin (1970a) reported the following experiment: subjects were shown a series of lists containing either five or 20 common words. A subject might, for example, see a five-word list, followed by a 20-word list, followed by another 20-word list, then a 5-word list, etc. The subjects had to recall all of the words from the list just preceding the most recent list presented. In the example given above, the subject first saw a 5-word list, then a 20-word list, and then attempted to recall the five-word list. Call this the 5–20 condition. Other conditions are therefore 5–5, 20–5, and 20–20, where the first number denotes the length of the list to be recalled and the second number denotes the length of the list intervening between presentation and recall of the list.

Although interference theory is designed to cover a somewhat different set of experimental paradigms, one can speculate about the predictions the theory makes about Shiffrin's experiment. One prediction is that the size of the intervening list should be critical. The longer the intervening list, the more it should interfere with what is to be recalled, because (a) there is more time for unlearning of the items in the earlier list to be recalled, and (b) there are more items in a longer intervening list that may compete with the items in the earlier list. Recall should therefore be poorer in the 5–20 and the 20–20 conditions because these have the long intervening lists. A retrieval failure theory makes a different prediction. Only the size of the list to be recalled should affect performance. The reason is that the subject is thought to use some sort of cue to locate the list to be recalled. The 20-word lists have larger search sets, and so there is a greater chance that once the list is located, a "stop rule" can be applied before a very large proportion of the items in the list can be found (Shiffrin, 1970b).

The results of Shiffrin's (1970a) experiment are shown in Table 4.2: Recall is determined by the length of the list to be recalled and is independent of the length of the intervening list, just as predicted by a retrieval failure theory. For some reason that neither we nor Shiffrin can explain, a longer intervening list results in slightly higher recall, but the effect is so small that it is probably caused by chance factors.

TABLE 4.2
Proportions of Words Correctly Recalled in the
Shiffrin (1970a) Experiment[a]

		Number of Words in the Intervening List	
		5	20
Size of to-be-	5	.33	.38
Recalled List	20	.10	.15

[a] Adapted from Shiffrin (1970a).

Although Shiffrin's experiment may appear to be a failure for interference theory, we reiterate that the theory has been designed to cover different situations. One must always be careful when attempting to apply a theory to a new situation, for one may make erroneous predictions that the proponents of the theory can never make. Although there are a number of findings that are bothersome to interference theory, the theory is still very much alive today. It has had an experimental history filled with empirical successes and failure. The failures have not bothered two of the theory's greatest proponents, Leo Postman and Benton Underwood; they view the theory as a "conceptual framework in continuing need of critical reexamination; . . . the most urgent task is the resolution of the many inconsistencies and apparent contradictions in the rapidly growing body of experimental findings" (Postman & Underwood, 1973, p. 37).

SUMMARY

This chapter has dealt with several aspects of information in long-term store. We have begun by discussing ways in which new information enters the store, emphasizing the importance of both rehearsal and organization. Next, we have concerned ourselves with the type of information that is stored in long-term store, concluding that at least two types of information, semantic and acoustic, are stored. Finally, we have taken up the topic of forgetting, an experience all of us have had at one time or another. Two explanations for forgetting are described: (1) interference theory and (2) retrieval failure. Both of these explanations contribute something to our understanding of the process of forgetting from long-term store.

5

Recognition Memory

Suppose you want to call up your friend, Joe Shablotnik, in New York City. To get Joe's number, you dial New York information and make your request, whereupon to your chagrin the operator informs you that there are two Joe Shablotniks in New York. To clarify the issue, she asks what street your Joe lives on. Unfortunately, you can't recall this information but, collecting your wits, you ask the operator for the addresses of both Joe Shablotniks. When the operator informs you that one Joe Shablotnik lives on Park Avenue, and the other Joe Shablotnik lives on Avenue D, you are instantly able to tell her that it is the Avenue D Joe Shablotnik that you want. Although you were not able to *recall* Joe's address, you were able to *recognize* it.

Up to this point, we have discussed memory without any particular regard to how memory performance has been measured. For the most part, we have talked about experiments in which a recall test is used. For example, in the Brown–Peterson short-term memory paradigm, the subject is asked to recall a triad of words or letters. Likewise, in a free-recall or serial-learning task, a subject is asked to recall and produce some information from memory. However, we know that in many everyday situations, the presence of some information in memory is tested not by recall, but by recognition; a person is presented with some stimulus and asked simply whether he has ever seen the stimulus before. One such situation is the address example given above. Another common situation is when you bump into a person at a party and you believe that you have seen him before (that is, you recognize the face even though you may not be able to recall the name).

TYPES OF RECOGNITION TESTS

To study recognition memory in the laboratory, two types of procedures are generally used: yes–no and forced-choice procedures (analogous to the true–false and multiple-choice tests that you used to take in high school).

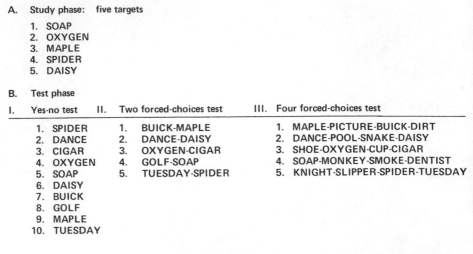

A. **Study phase:** five targets

1. SOAP
2. OXYGEN
3. MAPLE
4. SPIDER
5. DAISY

B. **Test phase**

I. Yes-no test   II. Two forced-choices test   III. Four forced-choices test

Yes-no test	Two forced-choices test	Four forced-choices test
1. SPIDER	1. BUICK-MAPLE	1. MAPLE-PICTURE-BUICK-DIRT
2. DANCE	2. DANCE-DAISY	2. DANCE-POOL-SNAKE-DAISY
3. CIGAR	3. OXYGEN-CIGAR	3. SHOE-OXYGEN-CUP-CIGAR
4. OXYGEN	4. GOLF-SOAP	4. SOAP-MONKEY-SMOKE-DENTIST
5. SOAP	5. TUESDAY-SPIDER	5. KNIGHT-SLIPPER-SPIDER-TUESDAY
6. DAISY		
7. BUICK		
8. GOLF		
9. MAPLE		
10. TUESDAY		

FIGURE 5.1   Types of recognition tests.

Figure 5.1 shows how these two procedures work. We can imagine a typical recognition-memory experiment as being divided into two phases, a study phase and a test phase. In the study phase, a number of stimuli (for example, single words) are presented to a subject. These stimuli seen at study are referred to as *target stimuli*. The nature of the test phase then depends on the type of recognition procedure being used. In a yes–no recognition test, the target stimuli are randomly permuted and then randomly intermingled with some number of *distractor stimuli* that did not appear during the study phase. The resultant set of targets and distractors are presented to the subject one by one. To each stimulus, the subject is requested to respond "Old" (if he thinks it is a target) or "New" (if he thinks it is a distractor). Conversely, in a forced-choice recognition test, each target stimulus is presented along with some number of distractor stimuli. In the example of Figure 5.1, instances are shown in which the target is presented with one or with three other distractors. These are referred to as two-alternative and four-alternative forced-choice recognition tests, respectively. On each trial the subject attempts to correctly pick the target out of the set of possible alternatives.

RECALL VERSUS RECOGNITION: LEVEL OF PERFORMANCE

A very old and stable finding is that, given some information stored in memory, a recognition test on the information leads to better performance (in terms of response probability) than a recall test (MacDougall, 1904; Postman,

Jenkins, & Postman, 1948; Postman, 1950). Most people are aware of this phenomenon in everyday life. Students taking tests know very well that they do better if the test is true–false or multiple choice (recognition) than if it is essay or fill in the blank (recall). There are three major reasons why recognition is better than recall.

Guessing rates. Suppose I ask you to "recall" the capital of Albania. Chances are that you are unable to do this; that is, on a recall test your memory performance on this information is virtually zero. A recognition test of the same information, however, may produce quite a different result. In particular, suppose I present you with the two alternatives

a. TIRANA

b. DURAZZO

and ask you to recognize which is the capital of Albania. Your likelihood of performing correctly on this test is now at least 50%, because you have a 50% chance of answering the question correctly by chance alone.

Complete versus discriminative information. The second reason for recognition superiority stems from the fact that performance on a recognition as opposed to a recall test may be based on somewhat different kinds of information. This can be seen from a common-sense point of view. To perform a recall test, a person needs more or less "complete" information about the stimulus remembered. For example, suppose you are trying to remember the word "silver." It does not help you a great deal in this enterprise to have partial information, to know that the word you are trying to recall refers to a metal or an element. To recognize some stimulus, however, you only need as much information as is necessary to *discriminate* the target stimulus from the distractor stimuli. For example, if you are given a two forced-choice recognition test in which "silver" is paired with "house," knowing any number of things about the target stimulus permits you to correctly perform the recognition task. Remembering that the target is a metal or that it is shiny or that it has something to do with coins can all do the trick.

An important corollary to this argument is that the more similar the targets are to the distractors, the more difficult is the recognition task. In the example above, we have seen that silver–house is an easy discrimination. However, if we use "copper" as a distractor in place of "house" the information mentioned above—that the target is a metal or shiny or has something to do with coins—is not sufficient to perform the recognition task (because copper shares these attributes). Experiments by Underwood (1965) and by Anisfeld and Knapp (1968) provide nice evidence for this notion. In these experiments, target–distractor similarity was systematically varied and, in general, the higher the target–distractor similarity, the poorer was the performance. In the area of picture memory an unpublished experiment performed by Harold McCoy at the University of Washington in 1974 has made the same point. McCoy's study phase used a series of related pictures, all of which involved a person shopping at a market. If the distractors consisted of other pictures of the same person doing his shopping, error rate was around 30%. If the distractor pictures were unrelated to the shopping trip, however, error rate dropped to about 1%.

Thus, performance on a recognition test may often be enhanced if obviously incorrect alternatives can be eliminated from consideration. To go back to our example of trying to recognize the name of the capital of Albania, suppose that instead of the alternatives TIRANA and DURAZZO, the alternatives were TIRANA and BOSTON. In this case a person would almost invariably choose the correct answer, TIRANA. That is because even people who have no idea what the capital of Albania is do know that Albania is extremely unlikely to have a capital named BOSTON. Admittedly, this example is a little extreme; however, anyone who has ever taken a multiple-choice test (such as college boards) knows that many questions have alternatives that may be safely eliminated as obviously incorrect.

Memory search.   Many theorists (for example, Kintsch, 1968, 1970a, b; Anderson & Bower, 1972) consider the act of recall to be composed of two major subprocesses. These processes are depicted in Figure 5.2. First, memory must be searched in an effort to locate the desired information. In the situation shown in Figure 5.2, the subject searches through long-term store trying to find potential candidates for words that have been on the list. Once a candidate has

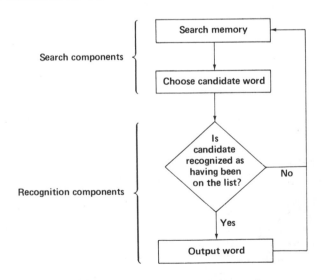

FIGURE 5.2   Processes involved in recall.

been located, a recognition test must be performed on it to ascertain whether it is a correct candidate. If a candidate is indeed recognized, then it is given as a response; otherwise, it is rejected and search continues.

In a recognition test, only the second component of the process is necessary; no memory search is needed because the correct information is directly available to the subject. In previous chapters, the notion of a retrieval cue has been discussed. A retrieval cue is some information provided by the experimenter at the time of the test (for example, a category name) that aids the subject in judiciously directing his search. A recognition test may be thought of as a situation in which the best possible retrieval cue, the desired information itself, is provided to the subject. It should therefore be clear that a recall test simultaneously tests whether information is stored in memory and also whether adequate retrieval paths to the information have been constructed. Recognition, however, may be viewed as a relatively "pure" measure of whether some information has been stored in memory; it is a test that is relatively uncontaminated by variations in the retrieval process.

One experimental situation in which the dichotomy between memory search and information recognition is illustrated quite dramatically is called a *feeling of knowing* experiment (Hart, 1967; Blake, 1973). Figure 5.3 shows how this sort of experiment works. The subject is first asked to recall some information In the example of Figure 5.3 (which depicts an experiment performed numerous times as a demonstration in G. Loftus' experimental psychology course) the subject is played part of an old song and is asked to recall the name of the

Each trial consists of

1. Play a 15-second cut of a song:
   "If you're going to San Francisco,
   Be sure to wear some flowers in your hair..."

2. Subject attempts to recall the singer:
   "...uh...Elvis?...no...Steve someone?...no, ummm..."

3. Subject rates how confident he is of being able to *recognize* the name of the singer:
   1 = Very confident
   2 = Moderately confident
   3 = Not at all confident

4. Subject is given a three forced-choice recognition test:
   a. Scott MacKenzie
   b. Niel Sedaka
   c. Paul Anka

5. Subject gives his recognition response:
   "AHA! It's (a), Scott MacKenzie. (I knew it all along)"

FIGURE 5.3   A "feeling of knowing" experiment.

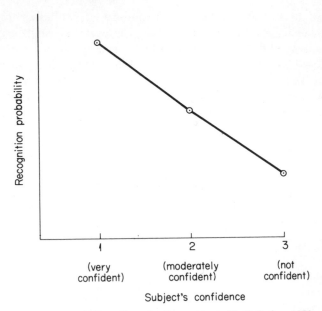

FIGURE 5.4   Results of the "feeling of knowing" experiment. (G. R. Loftus, 1972, unpublished.)

singer. If this information cannot be recalled, the subject is then asked to rate (on a scale from 1 to 3) how confident he feels of being able to *recognize* the name of the singer in a three forced-choice recognition test. The final component consists of actually giving the recognition test. Figure 5.4 shows the results of this demonstration, plotting the probability of correctly recognizing the name as a function of the subject's confidence of being able to recognize it. The decreasing curve illustrates very well that subjects know what information they have stored even if they are not able to find it. Even if memory search ends in failure subjects know how well they are likely to perform on a recognition test for the same information.

A second, related situation that illustrates the dichotomy between memory search and recognition is the *"tip of the tongue" phenomenon*. This is a situation that has probably been experienced by everybody at one time or another. You are searching for some information (for example, the name of the male lead in the movie, "Mutiny on the Bounty") but you just can't come up with it. You may even have part of the information, such as the facts that the first name has one syllable and that the last name begins with G, but you can't put it all together (it's very frustrating). You know, however, that if someone presented the correct information as part of a recognition test, for example,

ERROL FLYNN
CLARK GABLE
HUMPHREY BOGART

you'd instantly be able to pick the correct answer. You also know that this capability has nothing to do with guessing rates or the ability to eliminate incorrect alternatives; even if somebody were to give you a list of 100 movie actors, you would still be able to scan through them and, with complete confidence, correctly identify Clark Gable. Once again, therefore, we have a situation in which recall is impossible because of memory search failure—but the information is known to be there. It can still be recognized instantly and without error.

OTHER RECALL–RECOGNITION DIFFERENCES

In the preceding section we have explored the bases of the most obvious difference between recognition and recall–recognition performance superiority. For quite some time it was believed that the advantage of recognition over recall was simply because recognition was an easier (more sensitive) test of the same information (Postman, 1963; Postman, Adams, & Phillips, 1955). However, more recent evidence suggests that recognition tests a different kind of memory than does recall (in line with the notions presented above that correct recognition requires different information than does correct recall). In particular, there are experimental variables that affect recognition and recall in quite different ways. We now turn to a discussion of some of these variables.

Stimulus frequency.   Consider an experiment in which a list of words, such as BOOK, AARDVARK, TABLE, and KUMQUAT is presented to a subject. One aspect of a word that is very important in determining whether or not it is remembered is the *frequency* with which that word occurs in everyday life. In the list presented above, BOOK and TABLE are high-frequency words, whereas AARDVARK and KUMQUAT are relatively low-frequency words. Various experiments have shown that high-frequency words are recalled a good deal better than low-frequency words; therefore, BOOK and TABLE are likely to be recalled a good deal better than AARDVARK and KUM-QUAT (for example, Bousfield & Cohen, 1955; Hall, 1954). However, the opposite holds true when a recognition test is used. When information is tested by recognition, low-frequency words are typically recognized better than high-frequency words (for example, Shepard, 1967; Gorman, 1961; Kinsbourne & George, 1974).

Incidental versus intentional learning.   Suppose a subject is presented with a list of words but he is not told that he will be required to remember them. Instead, he is simply asked to perform some innocuous task, such as rating each word for its "pleasantness." Following this procedure, the subject, to his surprise, is given a memory test that can be either recognition or recall. How does the subject's memory performance in this *incidental* condition

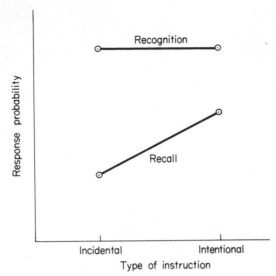

FIGURE 5.5   A comparison of recognition and recall memory in the incidental – intentional paradigm.

compare to his performance in a normal *intentional* condition in which the subject knew he would have to remember the words at the time he first saw them? Figure 5.5 shows the typical results (cf. Estes & DaPolito, 1967). Recall performance is drastically affected by the incidental–intentional manipulation; performance is considerably worse in the incidental condition. However, in general, recognition is either not affected at all by the manipulation or is actually better in the incidental condition.

An experiment by Woodward, Bjork, and Jongeward (1973) has added a new twist to the incidental learning paradigm. Figure 5.6 shows the design of this experiment. A series of trials was presented to a subject, each trial involving (1) presentation of a word for 1 second, (2) a rehearsal interval that varied from 0 to 12 seconds and (3) a recall test of the word. Not surprisingly, subjects were virtually perfect on this test. However, at the end of the series of trials, a final test was administered. Figure 5.7 shows the results of this test, plotting memory performance as a function of the rehearsal interval length. In line with our earlier discussion of maintenance versus elaborative rehearsal (Chapter 4) when a recall test was given, rehearsal interval length had no effect. Words that had been maintained in the rehearsal buffer for 12 seconds were recalled no better than words that had only been in the rehearsal buffer for 1 second. In contrast, if the final test was a recognition test, performance increased as a function of the rehearsal interval.

These results are interesting for two reasons. First, they replicate the finding that merely maintaining a word in short-term store does not necessarily boost

A. Each trial consists of

    1.   Presentation of a word

          APPLE

               Variable retention interval of 0-12 seconds

    2.   Subject is free to rehearse the word during this retention interval

    3.   Subject recalls word

          "Apple. (That was easy . . .)"

B. After all trials are done a surprise final test is given. This final test is either recall or recognition.

FIGURE 5.6   Design of the Woodward *et al.* (1973) experiment.

eventual recall performance on the word. Second, however, these results indicate that maintaining information in short-term store results in transfer of information to long-term store that is somehow useful for recognition. A tentative conclusion is that "elaboration" of information in short-term store results in the construction of retrieval paths that are useful for recall but not for recognition. Conversely, mere maintenance of information in short-term store results in an increase in "strength" of the information that is useful for recognition but not for recall.

Subject strategies. In our initial description of the Atkinson–Shiffrin memory model (Chapter 1) it has been pointed out that a number of information-processing options are under control of the subject. The decisions

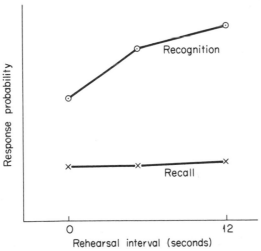

FIGURE 5.7   Results of the Woodward *et al.* (1973) experiment. (After Woodward *et al.*, 1973, Figure 7.)

of whether or not to enter some information into the rehearsal buffer, how much information to hold in the buffer at a given time, and how much information to transfer to long-term store per unit time are all examples of such control processes.

Given this situation, it seems reasonable to expect that subjects may use such control to process information differentially depending on whether they expect to be tested by recall or by recognition. For instance, students studying for an examination typically want to know whether the exam is to be true–false or multiple choice (recognition) or essay (recall). The implication is that the student's method of studying (processing the information) differs depending on the nature of the exam.

An experiment by Tversky (1973) provides evidence supporting this hypothesis. Tversky's procedure was simple. She presented a series of stimuli (pictures of common objects). Half the subjects in Tversky's experiment were told they were to be tested by recall, whereas the other half were told they would be tested by recognition. These two groups of subjects were further subdivided at the time of the test. Half the subjects in each group were actually given a recall test, whereas the other half were given a recognition test. Therefore, half the subjects were tested by the method they anticipated, whereas the other half were double crossed and tested by an unanticipated method.

Tversky's results (Figure 5.8) are very clear-cut. If a subject was tested by the anticipated method, his performance was higher on both types of tests than

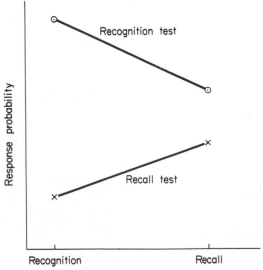

FIGURE 5.8   Results of the Tversky (1973) experiment. (Adapted from Tversky, 1973.)

if he was tested by an unanticipated method. Evidently, subjects do process information differently depending on how they expect to be tested on the information. Tversky's results indicate that "recall" processing is not appropriate for recognition and vice versa.

An experiment by G. R. Loftus (1971) investigated recall–recognition strategy differences within the context of the Atkinson–Shiffrin memory theory. Loftus used a paired-associate procedure and informed subjects as to whether they were to be tested by recall or by recognition. A mathematical procedure, called a parameter grid search, was then applied to the data, which allowed Loftus to estimate (1) how much information subjects were holding in short-term store during study, (2) how much information per unit time subjects were transferring to long-term store, and (3) about how much time any given item remained in short-term store. Table 5.1 shows the results of this analysis. When subjects knew they would be tested by recall, they tended to hold a relatively large amount of information (about three items) in short-term store at a given time and tranfer information to long-term store rather slowly. Conversely, when a recognition test was expected, only one item was held in short-term store at any given time, and a relatively large amount of information was transferred to long-term store over a short period of time. Note, however, that the *total* amount of information transferred to long-term store (defined as the average time information spent in short-term store multiplied by the transfer rate) was greater when a recall as opposed to a recognition test was expected.

TABLE 5.1
Results of the Loftus (1971) Experiment[a]

	Recognition	Recall
Amount of information held in short-term store (paired-associate items)	1	3
Amount of information per second transferred to long-term store (arbitrary units)	0.079	0.030
Amount of time a given item remains in short-term store (seconds)	10	30
Total amount of information transferred to long-term store (arbitrary units)	0.79	0.90

[a] Adapted from Loftus (1971).

These strategies are commensurate with the type of information needed for the two types of tests. Because recall requires rather complete information, a reasonable strategy is to maintain as many items as possible for as long as possible in short-term store, because complete information can be easily retrieved from short-term store. A recognition test, however, can be performed on the basis of sketchy, incomplete information in long-term store; it therefore makes sense to send off a good deal of information about each item to long-term store without worrying about maintaining complete information in short-term store.

THEORIES OF RECOGNITION MEMORY

The fact that recognition differs in so many ways from recall has led to the construction of models and theories strictly designed to handle recognition. In this section, we shall discuss two of these models: the "all-or-none" and the "signal-detection" models. For simplicity, we shall restrict our discussion to the simplest type of recognition memory—yes–no recognition (cf. Swets, 1964, for a discussion of how these models are extended to other types of recognition).

Memory strength and criterion. In a yes–no recognition test, we actually have two things to worry about. Figure 5.9 illustrates why this is so. Figure 5.9a shows a situation in which a subject is read ten two-digit target numbers in a study phase. In the test phase, the subject is presented the ten

Study phase:	(1) 13	(2) 47	(3) 43	(4) 73	(5) 86
(10 items)	(6) 97	(7) 74	(8) 24	(9) 67	(10) 62
Test phase:	(1) 74	(2) 67	(3) 16	(4) 73	(5) 76
(yes-no	(6) 22	(7) 43	(8) 62	(9) 77	(10) 86
recogni-	(11) 94	(12) 39	(13) 47	(14) 84	(15) 70
tion test)	(16) 29	(17) 13	(18) 74	(19) 17	(20) 97

For any given test item there are four possible outcomes:

Correct response

	Old	New
Old	Hit (correct) 8 items	False alarm (incorrect) 4 items
New	Miss (incorrect) 2 items	Correct rejection (correct) 6 items
	10 items in all	10 items in all

FIGURE 5.9   Types of responses in a yes–no recognition test.

target numbers along with ten distractors in a yes–no recognition test. On a test trial, one of four different outcomes can occur, as depicted in Figure 5.9b. First, the test item can be either a target or a distractor. Second, for both these cases, the subject may respond either "Old" or "New." As can easily be seen, of these four outcomes, two outcomes are correct (responding "Old" to a target and responding "New" to a distractor). The other two responses (responding "Old" to a distractor and responding "New" to a target) are incorrect. Each of these four possible outcomes has a name, as shown in Figure 5.9b. Of particular interest are "hits" (correctly responding "Old" to a target item) and "false alarms" (incorrectly responding "Old" to a distractor item). In the example, the subject has made eight hits and four false alarms. Notice that by knowing the number of hits and false alarms, we can immediately calculate the number of misses and correct rejections. Because there have been ten targets and hits have been made on eight of them, misses must have been made on the other two. Likewise, because there have been ten distractors, and false alarms have been made on four of them, correct rejections must have been made on the other six. By knowing about hits and false alarms, we therefore, have all the information we need to characterize performance. Finally, by dividing the number of hits and false alarms by the numbers of targets and distractors, respectively, we obtain the hit *probability* $(8/10 = .8)$ and the false-alarm probability $(4/10 = .4)$. It is these probabilities with which the models deal.

Notice now that "high memory strength" would imply a high hit probability and a low false-alarm probability—for example, if memory were perfect, the hit probability would be 1.0 and the false-alarm probability would be 0. Notice also, however, that no matter how good or bad your memory strength was, it would be possible to have either a very high hit probability *or* a very low false-alarm probability (although not necessarily both). For example, a subject could, if he wished, respond "Old" to all the test stimuli. In this case, his hit probability would be 1.0, but his false-alarm probability would also be 1.0, and his overall probability correct would be at the chance rate of 50%. At the other extreme, a subject could respond "New" to all stimuli, in which case his false-alarm probability would be 0, but his hit probability would also be 0—and his overall probability correct would again be at the chance level of 50%.

Whereas subjects are typically not so extreme in their responding, the above discussion should serve to introduce the notion of a *criterion* for responding old or new, a criterion that is under the control of the subject. A very "conservative" subject may require a large amount of evidence before declaring a test stimulus to be old; such a subject is likely to respond "Old" very seldom and therefore to have a very low hit probability but also a low false-alarm probability. A "liberal" subject (with exactly the same information in his memory) may, in contrast, require very little evidence before calling something

Defendent is actually:

		Guilty	Innocent
Judge's decision:	Convict	Correct decision (analogous to a hit)	Incorrect decision (analogous to a false alarm)
	Acquit	Incorrect decision (analogous to a miss)	Correct decision (analogous to a correct rejection)

FIGURE 5.10   Possible outcomes of a judge's decision.

old. This subject would say "Old" frequently and have a high hit probability but also a high false-alarm probability.

Before this criterion issue is abandoned, it may be useful to provide an analogy. Consider the task of a judge who must either acquit or convict a defendant of some crime. Figure 5.10 shows four possible outcomes of the judge's decision. Here, convicting a guilty person is analogous to a hit, whereas convicting an innocent person is analogous to a false alarm. Two factors go into the judge's decision. The first factor is the *evidence* that the person is innocent or guilty. The second factor is the judge's *criterion* for how much evidence he requires to convict. A judge may be very *lenient*, in which case he rarely convicts an innocent person—but he may erroneously acquit a lot of people who are actually guilty. Conversely, the judge may be a "hanging judge"—one shred of evidence and the defendant is declared to be guilty. A hanging judge rarely acquits a guilty person but he may erroneously convict many innocent people.

Bearing in mind that a model of recognition memory must handle both of these factors, response strength and criterion, let us turn now to a discussion of how recognition memory is viewed as an all-or-none process.

An all-or-none model.   For a long time, theories of recognition memory assumed that when target items were studied, each item was learned in an all-or-none fashion (for example, Hilgard, 1951). Suppose we designate the probability that a target item is learned at the time of the study by $p(L)$. It is now $p(L)$ which is of interest to us as a measure of "memory strength," and we shall want to see how it is affected by such variables as study time, study conditions, and type of stimulus material. Figure 5.11 gives an example of how $p(L)$ may be calculated from the hit and false-alarm probabilities, often referred to as $p(H)$ and $p(FA)$, respectively. Suppose $p(L)$ is, in fact, equal to 0.6; of the ten targets shown at study, therefore, six of them are learned. The ten distractors are certainly unlearned; but nevertheless, the subject says "Old" to some of them anyway. The proportion of distractor items to which the subject responds old is, of course, the false alarm probability, $p(FA)$. In Figure 5.11, the subject responds "Old" to five of the ten distractors, and the false alarm

Study phase: present ten targets

1.	T1		7.	T7	
2.	T2		8.	T8	Unlearned
3.	T3	Learned	9.	T9	
4.	T4		10.	T10	
5.	T5				
6.	T6				

Test phase: present ten targets and ten distractors. (In an actual experiment, targets and distractors would be randomly intermixed)

	Targets				Distractors		
Item	State of learning	Response	Type of outcome	Item	State of learning	Response	Type of outcome[a]
T1	Learned	"old"	Hit	D1	Unlearned	"new"	
T2	Learned	"old"	Hit	D2	Unlearned	"old"	FA
T3	Learned	"old"	Hit	D3	Unlearned	"new"	
T4	Learned	"old"	Hit	D4	Unlearned	"old"	FA
T5	Learned	"old"	Hit	D5	Unlearned	"new"	
T6	Learned	"old"	Hit	D6	Unlearned	"old"	FA
T7	Unlearned	"new"		D7	Unlearned	"new"	
T8	Unlearned	"old"	Hit	D8	Unlearned	"old"	FA
T9	Unlearned	"new"		D9	Unlearned	"new"	
T10	Unlearned	"old"	Hit	D10	Unlearned	"old"	FA

[a] FA = false alarm

FIGURE 5.11   Logic of an all-or-none recognition model

probability is therefore 0.5. Of the ten targets, we know that the subject responds "Old" to the six that are in the learned state. What about the other four targets? They are unlearned, so they are in the same state as distractors—and we know from the false-alarm rate that the subject responds "Old" to an item in the unlearned state with a probability of .5. We therefore expect the subject to respond "Old" to two of the four unlearned targets. In all, he responds "Old" to eight targets, giving him a hit rate of $8/10 = .8$.

To generalize this example and express it in terms of simple mathematics, we are assuming that $p(H)$ is equal to the proportion of learned items, $p(L)$, plus the proportion of unlearned items, $[1 - p(L)]$ times $p(FA)$, or

(5.1) $$p(H) = p(L) + [1 - p(L)]p(FA).$$

Now, using algebra, we solve for $p(L)$ to obtain

(5.2) $$p(L) = \frac{p(H) - p(FA)}{1 - p(FA)}.$$

Or, to estimate $p(L)$ from data, we simple take $p(H)$ and $p(FA)$ and plug them into Equation (5.2).

The crucial thing to notice in this equation is that memory strength is related to the *difference* between the hit and false-alarm probabilities. If the hit probability exceeds the false alarm probability by a substantial amount, memory strength is estimated to be large. In contrast, if the hit and false-alarm probabilities are very close to each other, memory strength is estimated to be low.

Although this model of recognition memory has an appealing simplicity, it is probably not very accurate in most situations. Intuitively, it seems unlikely that a fairly complex stimulus, such as a word that can be encoded in a myriad of different ways, is either completely learned or not learned at all. Logically, it does not make very much sense that an item is learned in an all-or-none way when "learning" is completely dependent on the similarity of the distractors (as we have seen in a previous section). Empirically, moreover, there is good evidence against the all-or-none model in the form of something called a *memory operating characteristic* (or MOC) curve. Figure 5.12 illustrates what an MOC curve is and where it comes from. The first thing to consider is that, given a certain amount of memory strength, we can experimentally manipulate

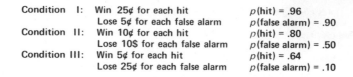

Condition	I:	Win 25¢ for each hit	p(hit) = .96
		Lose 5¢ for each false alarm	p(false alarm) = .90
Condition	II:	Win 10¢ for each hit	p(hit) = .80
		Lose 10$ for each false alarm	p(false alarm) = .50
Condition	III:	Win 5¢ for each hit	p(hit) = .64
		Lose 25¢ for each false alarm	p(false alarm) = .10

(a)

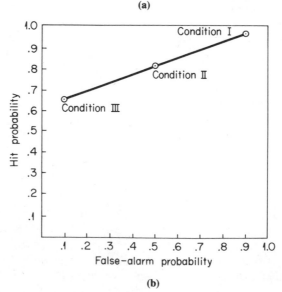

(b)

FIGURE 5.12   Memory operating characteristic (MOC) curves: (a) construction of an MOC curve as predicted by an all-or-none model of recognition memory; (b) the MOC curve predicted by an all-or-none model.

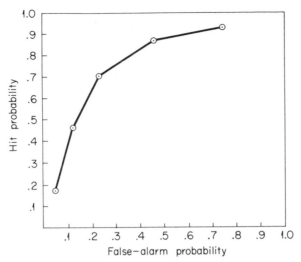

FIGURE 5.13 An empirical MOC curve.

a subject's hit and false-alarm rates by inducing him to change his criterion for responding "Old." There are many ways of doing this. In the example of Figure 5.12, this is done by varying the *payoff structure*. The hypothetical experiment has three conditions that involve three different payoff structures. In Condition I, which pays 25¢ for a hit but only charges a nickel for a false-alarm, a smart subject should say "Old" to almost everything. Conversely, in Condition III, it costs the subject a quarter for every false-alarm, but only a nickel is paid for a hit; in this condition, therefore, the subject should respond "New" to almost everything in order to minimize his losses. Finally, Condition II is in between these two extremes.

For such an experiment, we can get hit and false-alarm probabilities for the three conditions and we can plot a function relating the two, which has been done at the bottom of Figure 5.12. This function is the MOC curve. It is worth emphasizing at this point that a given MOC curve depicts performance for a given amount of memory strength; each point on the curve represents a different criterion level and therefore different hit and false-alarm probabilities.

What form should the MOC curve take? A glance back at Equation (5.1) reveals that the all-or-none model predicts the function to be *linear* with a slope equal to $[1 - p(L)]$ and an intercept equal to $p(L)$. Therefore, the MOC curve of Figure 5.12 is an example of the kind of MOC curve predicted by the all-or-none model. However, empirical MOC curves do not typically look like this; instead, they are bow shaped as depicted in Figure 5.13. So the prediction of the model fails.

Number	Type[a]	Familiarity	Number	Type	Familiarity	Number	Type	Familiarity	Number	Type	Familiarity
1	T	13	31	D	-1	61	D	1	91	T	1
2	T	-1	32	T	8	62	T	4	92	T	6
3	D	-1	33	D	-9	63	T	3	93	D	-1
4	D	1	34	T	3	64	D	-5	94	T	9
5	T	5	35	T	7	65	T	6	95	D	0
6	D	-4	36	D	-1	66	D	3	96	D	-3
7	T	2	37	D	-4	67	D	-2	97	T	5
8	D	7	38	T	14	68	T	7	98	D	9
9	T	6	39	T	-1	69	T	0	99	D	5
10	D	-6	40	D	1	70	D	1	100	T	3
11	T	7	41	T	6	71	T	8	101	D	-1
12	D	2	42	D	-2	72	D	2	102	T	-2
13	D	3	43	T	4	73	D	-1	103	T	7
14	T	10	44	D	1	74	T	10	104	D	1
15	T	4	45	T	-4	75	T	5	105	D	2
16	T	9	46	T	7	76	D	-3	106	T	6
17	D	-4	47	D	0	77	D	-8	107	D	5
18	D	8	48	D	2	78	T	11	108	T	3
19	D	3	49	D	4	79	T	4	109	T	-1
20	T	4	50	D	3	80	D	-2	110	T	4
21	T	12	51	T	1	81	T	5	111	T	2
22	T	5	52	T	2	82	D	6	112	D	0
23	T	6	53	D	2	83	D	4	113	T	0
24	D	0	54	D	6	84	T	3	114	T	-3
25	D	0	55	D	-3	85	D	0	115	D	8
26	T	8	56	D	5	86	T	0	116	D	-6
27	D	4	57	T	-7	87	T	-3	117	T	9
28	D	5	58	T	6	88	D	1	118	T	1
29	T	11	59	D	0	89	D	4	119	T	5
30	D	2	60	T	5	90	D	-2	120	D	-2

[a]T = Target   D = Distractor.

FIGURE 5.14a

102

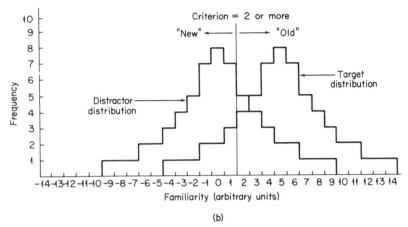

FIGURE 5.14   Assumptions of signal-detection theory: (a) familiarity of all test stimuli; (b) frequency distributions of familiarity for targets and distractors.

It turns out that the bow-shaped MOC curve can be predicted by a theory of recognition memory which assumes that information about a target item is acquired *continuously* as opposed to in an all-or-none fashion. It is to a description of this kind of model that we now turn.

A signal-detection model.   The theory of signal-detection was originally formulated to account for psychophysical data on detection of weak stimuli (Swets, Tanner, & Birdsall, 1961; Swets, 1964; Green & Swets, 1966). In the late 1950s and the 1960s, parts of the theory were modified in order to apply it to recognition memory data (Egan, 1958; Parks, 1966; Bernbach, 1967; Freund, Loftus, & Atkinson, 1969) and since then has been the predominant framework within which recognition data have been couched (Banks, 1970; Lockhart & Murdock, 1970).

Figure 5.14 illustrates the basic assumptions of signal-detection theory. The example shown in Figure 5.14 involves a typical yes–no recognition experiment with 60 targets and 60 distractors. The basic assumption is that any given test item has some amount of *familiarity*. The top half of Figure 5.14 lists the familiarity values associated with each of the 120 test items. Consider first the distractor items. The average (mean) familiarity value of the distractors is arbitrarily set at zero (this is an easy thing to do because the units of familiarity are arbitrary to begin with). However, not all distractors have a familiarity of exactly zero. Some have greater than zero familiarity, whereas others have less than zero familiarity, so there is what is termed a *distribution* of familiarity for the distractors around the mean of zero. Now consider the 60 target items. By virtue of having been seen at the time of study, the targets, in general, have a higher familiarity than the distractors. In the example of Figure 5.14, the mean familiarity of the targets turns out to be five. Again, however, not all targets have a value of exactly five—some have a value more than five; others have a value less than five.

At the bottom of Figure 5.14 are plotted the *frequency distributions* of familiarity for the targets and the distractors. These distributions have been constructed from the data at the top of Figure 5.14. For example, only one distractor (Number 33) has a familiarity value of −9, and two distractors (Numbers 54 and 82) have a familiarity value of 6. Likewise, only one target (Number 38) has a familiarity value of 14 and two targets (Numbers 29 and 78) have familiarity values of 11. Three targets (Numbers 16, 94, and 117) but only one distractor (Number 98) have familiarity values of 9, and so on. As can be seen, these distributions overlap to a certain extent; that is to say, some high-value distractors have a higher familiarity than some low-value targets.

How does a subject decide to respond "Old" or "New" to a given test item? The theory assumes that the subject sets a *criterion* familiarity value. If the familiarity of a given test item is above the criterion, the subject responds "Old"; otherwise, he responds "New." In the example of Figure 5.14, the subject has set his criterion familiarity at 2. A response of "Old" is therefore made to any test item with a familiarity of 2 or more, whereas a response of "New" is made to any test item with a familiarity less than 2. We can now easily determine the hit and false-alarm probabilities by looking at the distributions and the criterion. Of the 60 targets, 50 of them have a familiarity that exceeds the criterion. Because the subject correctly responds "Old" to these 50 targets, the hit rate is 50/60 or 0.83. Of the 60 distractors, however, 19 have familiarity values of 2 or more. Because the subject incorrectly responds "Old" to these items, the false-alarm rate is 19/60 or 0.32.

How is memory strength to be characterized within this signal-detection framework? Note that what is assumed to be happening during study is that the familiarity value of the target items is being increased. Accordingly, a good measure of strength is the amount of increase in familiarity, that is, the difference between the means of the distractor and the target distributions. This difference is denoted by d. In the example of Figure 5.14, $d = 5$.

In practice, a problem arises with simply using d as a strength measure. This is because the units of familiarity are arbitrary, so it is impossible to compare d across different experiments; that is, d has no intrinsic meaning. To solve this problem, d is typically expressed as a *standard score*—it is the difference between the two means divided by the standard deviation of the distractor distribution. This standard measure is called d', which is the strength measure typically used in recognition-memory experiments. There are various ways to compute d' from the hit and false-alarm probabilities. The easiest way is to look it up in tables that have been prepared by Elliott (1964).

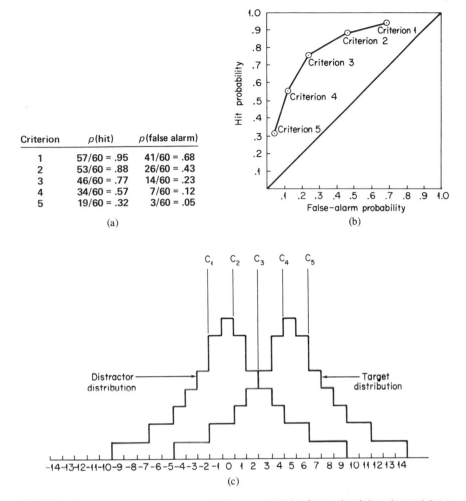

Criterion	p(hit)	p(false alarm)
1	57/60 = .95	41/60 = .68
2	53/60 = .88	26/60 = .43
3	46/60 = .77	14/60 = .23
4	34/60 = .57	7/60 = .12
5	19/60 = .32	3/60 = .05

(a)

FIGURE 5.15 Memory operating characteristic curve prediction from a signal-detection model: (a) hit and false-alarm probabilities corresponding to different criteria; (b) the derived MOC curve; (c) the distractor and target familiarity distributions along with the five criteria.

Figure 5.15 illustrates why a signal-detection model predicts the bow-shaped MOC curve. The distractor and target distributions from Figure 5.14 have been redrawn at the bottom of Figure 5.15. Five criterion levels are shown, and in the top left-hand part of the figure are listed the hit and false-alarm probabilities for these five criteria. Finally, in the top right-hand part of the figure, these hit and false-alarm probabilities are plotted against each other. As can easily be seen, the resulting MOC curve takes on the bow form originally depicted in Figure 5.13.

SUMMARY

We began this chapter by discussing the nature of recognition tests in contrast to recall tests. It was pointed out that a recognition test typically yields superior performance for three reasons. First, guessing probability is higher in a recognition test. Second, correct recognition may be carried out simply because incorrect alternatives can be easily rejected. And finally, recall involves a memory search, whereas recognition probably does not require such a search.

Recognition and recall tests probably tap different types of memory. Evidence for this contention stems from the fact that certain experimental variables (for example, stimulus frequency; incidental versus intentional learning) affect recall and recognition performance in opposite ways.

Two models of recognition memory have been used in the past: an all-or-none model and a signal-detection (continuous) model. The available evidence suggests that of the two, the signal-detection model is probably the more accurate; and this model forms the underlying framework for most current work in recognition memory.

6

Long-Term Memory for Meaningful Material

On Friday, July 13, 1973, the Seattle Times printed the article shown in Figure 6.1. Suppose you read the Times in the morning and later that day a friend asked you what the paper said about Nixon. What would you say? You would probably have answered something like "Nixon's in the hospital with pneumonia. It's not too serious because he's going to keep working." Your friend would be most surprised, however, if you responded "President Nixon intends to carry on the essential work of his office while in the hospital with viral pneumonia, the White House said today. Press Secretary Ronald L. Ziegler said Mr. Nixon was champing at the bit to keep working. . . ."

No one expects a verbatim story. It is only in rare instances, such as memorizing lines for a play, that we must remember things word for word. In our everyday life, we don't remember all the information that we perceive; we remember only a selected portion of it. When we read a newspaper, we don't

WASHINGTON — (AP) — President Nixon intends to carry on "the essential work of his office" while in the hospital with viral pneumonia, the White House said today.

Press Secretary Ronald L. Ziegler said Mr. Nixon was "champing at the bit" to keep working while doctors sought to cut down his schedule to less than a quarter of normal presidential activity.

Doctors said they expected the President, who was admitted last night, to remain at Bethesda Naval Medical Center from seven to 10 days. Visitors were being kept to an absolute minimum.

At a briefing this morning, the doctors said Mr. Nixon was running a temperature of from 101 to 102 degrees and was attended by four doctors. He received an analgesic injection so he could get some sleep after a restless first night at the hospital, they said.

Dr. Walter Tkach, White House physician, said that all the doctors on the case agree that aside from the viral pneumonia, the President had no other illness or complication.

However, Dr. Tkach said a viral illness weakens the patient and therefore he would estimate "another week to 10 days of hospitalization."

FIGURE 6.1 Newspaper clipping from *The Seattle Times*, July 13, 1973. What do you remember after a single reading?

107

remember exactly how the stories were worded; we remember only the general theme of what they said. This chapter deals with the question of what happens when a person sees or hears a sentence, paragraph, or a passage of meaningful material (sometimes called *ordinary* or *connected discourse*). We already know that he performs a number of initial operations on the material, such as pattern recognition, that result in the attachment of meaning to the material. However, in this chapter we are primarily interested what he *remembers* of the material later on.

FORM VERSUS MEANING

Fillenbaum (1966) presented subjects with a long list of such sentences as "The door was not closed" and later tested them on their memory for the sentences. At the time subjects originally saw the sentences, they did not know exactly how they would be tested. In fact, the test was a four-alternative recognition test in which subjects had to choose the sentence they had heard earlier. The incorrect alternatives were systematically related to the original sentence in terms of form and meaning. A test for the above sentence would look like this:

Alternative	Relationship to correct alternative
a. The door was not open.	Similar form, opposite meaning
b. The door was not closed.	Correct alternative
c. The door was closed.	Dissimilar form, opposite meaning
d. The door was open.	Dissimilar form, same meaning

Of interest in the experiment was which alternative the subject would choose if he did not choose the correct Alternative b. It was not expected that he would choose Alternative c, which was dissimilar in meaning *and* form. So the question was: would he remember meaning at the expense of form and choose Alternative d? Or would he remember form at the expense of meaning and choose Alternative a? The results were clear-cut. If the subject failed to choose the correct alternative, he was much more likely to choose the similar meaning Alternative d than to choose one that was more similar in form (Alternative a). The results of this very simple experiment therefore suggest that subjects had encoded the meaning of the sentences at the expense of the form or wording of the sentence.

Before we proceed with additional evidence on the form versus meaning issue, however, we interject a note of caution about the methodology being used. Some linguists and psychologists (for example, the Harvard linguist Dwight Bolinger) have argued strongly that active/passive form and meaning cannot really be separated. When you change form, they claim, you often change meaning. As we have just seen, Fillenbaum (1966) has changed the form of a sentence by changing it from active to passive or vice versa. When a subject recognizes the change, it is assumed that he can recognize form changes and must therefore have stored some information about form in long-term store. However, it is possible that in changing a sentence from active to passive, the meaning of the sentence is changed somewhat. This is most obvious with idioms: "He kicked the bucket" does not mean the same thing as the passive "The bucket was kicked by him." The point still holds with nonidiomatic sentences: Whereas "The stranger approached me" can be turned into "I was approached by the stranger" with no trouble, "The train approached me" does not become "I was approached by the train" without sounding comical. The major point of these examples is that when we change the form of a sentence we must be careful that we are not also changing its meaning.

Integration of meaning over time.   Returning to the issue of whether we remember form or meaning, Bransford and Franks (1971) have also presented subjects with a list of sentences. Here, however, the sentences are elements of a story. An example of four sentences making up a story is the following:

1. The rock rolled down the mountain.
2. The rock crushed the hut.
3. The hut is at the river.
4. The hut is tiny.

The story can also be expressed by a single sentence that contains all four elements: "The rock that rolled down the mountain crushed the tiny hut at the river."

In Bransford and Franks' experiment, subjects saw a series of sentences containing one, two, or three elements. An example of a two-element sentence is "The tiny hut is at the river" and an example of a three-element sentence is "The rock crushed the tiny hut at the river." Of critical importance is the fact that sentences were randomly intermixed with one-, two-, and three-element sentences from other stories. For example, the subjects might see, "The rock rolled down the mountain," then see three or four unrelated sentences, and then see "The rock crushed the tiny hut." To make sure that the subjects understood the sentences, they answered a simple question about each sentence immediately after it was presented. Then, about 5 minutes after all the sentences had been presented, the subjects were given a yes–no recognition test. They were shown one-, two-, and three-element test sentences that had been presented and one-, two-, three-, and four-element test sentences that had not been presented. Their task was to state whether or not they had heard each test sentence before and to state their confidence that they were correct. The basic result is shown in Figure 6.2. The more elements of the story a test sentence contained, the more confident a subject was that he had heard the sentence before. Notice that subjects were most confident that they had heard

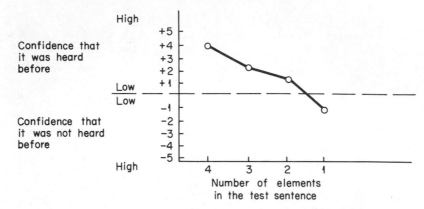

FIGURE 6.2 Confidence that a test sentence had been heard before, for various types of sentences. The more elements of the whole story that a sentence contained, the more confident the subject was that he had heard it before. Subjects were most confident about the four element sentence, which had never even been presented. (After Bransford & Franks, 1971.)

the sentence containing four elements, a sentence that had never been presented to them. Amazingly, therefore, the subjects were more apt to think they had heard "The rock that rolled down the mountain crushed the tiny hut at the river" (which in fact they had *never* heard) than "The rock that rolled down the mountain crushed the tiny hut" (which in fact they had heard).

These findings imply that when the subjects initially hear the one-, two-, and three-element sentences, they somehow abstract the entire story and store it in memory, rather than store the exact wording. This is why the story in its complete four-element form looked familiar to the subjects even though they had never seen the story in that form before. The Bransford–Franks' experiment is important in that it can shed some light on how it is we sometimes "remember" something that has never even occurred.

A real-life setting.   One possible problem with the Fillenbaum and Bransford–Franks techniques was that subjects knew that the materials to be remembered were stimuli in a memory experiment. Therefore, they might not have treated the material as they would have treated ordinary, everyday discourse. Wanner (1968) devised a technique that avoids this problem. In Wanner's experiments, the subjects first heard instructions, presented via taperecorder, telling them the procedure of the experiment. After the procedure had been outlined, the subjects were told that they would be asked to score their own answers when the experiment was finished. They were told something such as "When you score your results mark carefully those answers that are wrong but do nothing to your correct answers." At this point, a deception was revealed: instead of the experiment's proceeding, memory for the instructions themselves was tested. The test consisted of showing the subjects two sentences, one of which had been presented in the instructions and the other of which had not. For half the subjects the distractor sentence was changed by altering word order but not changing meaning; for the remaining subjects the altered word order did change the meaning. Suppose, for example, that Sentence 1 (below) represents a sentence that had originally been heard in the instructions. Sentence 2 is a sentence with altered word order but the same meaning, whereas Sentence 3 has had the meaning changed:

1. When you score your results mark carefully those answers which are wrong but do nothing to your correct answers.
2. When you score your results carefully mark those answers which are wrong but do nothing to your correct answers.
3. When you score your results mark carefully those answers which are wrong but do nothing to correct your answers.

In Sentence 2 the order of "mark" and "carefully" has been altered, but no change in meaning results. In Sentence 3 the order of "correct" and "your" has been altered, and a change in meaning does result. "Your correct" means do not mark your correct answers, whereas "correct your" means do not cheat by altering your incorrect answers.

Subjects could accurately recognize changes that altered meaning but were poor at recognizing changes that did not. These subjects did not expect to be tested on the material in the instructions; they presumably processed the instructions simply to comprehend them normally, and they remembered nothing about their wording, retaining only their gist.

The basic generalization from such results as those of Fillenbaum, Bransford and Franks, and Wanner is that the stored representation of sentences and ordinary discourse is semantic.

A test with warning. The preceding examples illustrate that under ordinary circumstances, subjects do not store information about the wording or form of sentences. In these experiments, however, subjects did not know they were to be tested for wording. Let us consider an experiment in which subjects were warned in advance that they must recognize changes in wording. The study has been performed by Sachs (1967). Subjects listened to stories in which a critical active or passive sentence had been embedded. The following story is an example.

There is an interesting story about the telescope. In Holland, a man named Lippershey was an eye-glass maker. One day his children were playing with some lenses. They discovered that things seemed very close if two lenses were held about a foot apart. Lippershey began experimenting and his "spyglass" attracted much attention. He sent a letter about it to Galileo, the great Italian scientist. Galileo at once realized the importance of the discovery and set about to build an instrument of his own. He used an old organ pipe with one lens curved out and the other in. On the first clear night he pointed the glass towards the sky. He was amazed to find the empty dark spaces filled with brightly gleaming stars . . . [p. 438].

Without looking back: which of these sentences did you see in the story?

1. He sent a letter about it to Galileo, the great Italian scientist.
2. Galileo, the great Italian scientist, sent him a letter about it.
3. A letter about it was sent to Galileo, the great Italian scientist.

The first sentence was the original sentence, the second sentence was changed in meaning, and the third sentence was changed in form (it became passive whereas the original was active). The subjects were tested either immediately after the critical sentence occurred, after a delay of 80 syllables, or after a delay of 160 syllables. (The test you just took incorporated a delay of 80 syllables.)

Sach's showed that with an immediate test, subjects were very likely to detect any changes in the sentence at all. This was to be expected because the subjects had just heard the sentence and might still have had an acoustic representation of it in short-term store. When tested at the 80- and 160-syllable delays, however, subjects' recognition of the form change was close to the chance level. Changes in the *meaning* of sentences however, were still recognized extremely well, and some of the changes were quite subtle. For example, after 80 syllables, seven out of eight subjects recognized the difference between these two sentences:

1. There he met an archaeologist, Howard Carter, who urged him to join in the search for the tomb of King Tut.
2. There he met an archaeologist, Howard Carter, and urged him to join in the search for the tomb of King Tut.

Therefore, even when subjects knew they would have to remember form, they were unable to do it. Meaning, however, was always well remembered.

An important exception.   Anderson and Bower's (1973, p. 224) results complicated the picture somewhat. Their subjects were shown a series of active and passive sentences. In one experiment, the sentences made up a story. In the second experiment, the same sentences were randomly presented and appeared to be a list of unrelated sentences. In one condition of these two experiments the subjects' memory for the critical sentences was tested after a delay of about 2 minutes. When asked to tell whether a critical sentence had been presented in the active or passive form, subjects in the "story" experiment were correct 56% of the time, not doing much better than a chance score of 50%. This result essentially replicated past findings. Subjects in the "unrelated" experiment, however, were correct in telling whether a critical sentence had been active or passive over 74% of the time, a value quite a bit higher than chance.

It therefore appears that in an "unrelated sentence" experiment where verbatim memory for surface features is emphasized, subjects can remember something about the form of the original sentences studied. In a "story" experiment, where a subject can get "lost" in the meaning, very little memory for form is evidenced.

This finding—that one result occurs when the material to be learned consists of a list of isolated, unrelated sentences, whereas another result occurs when the material to be learned consists of those same sentences in story form—is an extremely important finding because it indicates that different processes may be at work with meaningful material as opposed to list material. Perhaps subjects do not store information about voice when working with meaningful material, whereas they do store such information when working with list material. Whatever the difference, this example illustrates the danger of using results from studies with word lists to make generalizations and predictions about results from studies using more complex, meaningful material.

Form versus meaning: A summary.   Most of the evidence supports the idea that when given meaningful material to learn, we remember the gist of it much better than we remember the exact wording. If the material is not too "meaningful" (if it consists, for example, of a list of unrelated sentences) and we try hard to remember the exact wording, then we may retain some of the information about form. Wanner (1968) has also shown that when a subject tries, he can store more information about form than he does during normal comprehension, and Tieman (1971) has shown that a subject does not usually focus on exact wording but he can when he thinks it will help. What we do depends at least partly on the demands of the task we are asked to do.

RECONSTRUCTIVE PROCESSES

Everyone seems to remember with unusual clarity what he was doing on November 22, 1963, at the precise moment when he heard that President Kennedy was dead. The President was shot at 12:30 p.m., Dallas time, and the announcement that he was dead came at about 1:30 p.m. in the same time zone. It was 11:30 a.m. in California, 2:30 p.m. in New York, and 7:30 p.m. in London. Although the time of day for the New Yorker may have been different from the time of day for the Californian (one had probably just eaten lunch, whereas the other was about to go), the experience of the two when they try to recall the event is probably much the same.

Refabrication.   When we try to remember events that happened a long time ago, it is hard for us to be accurate. Sometimes we know a few facts, and using these we can construct other facts that probably happened. From these probable inferences we are led to other "facts," which were also probably true given that the foregoing facts were at least approximately true. To paraphrase C. S. Morgan (1917), we fill up the lowlands of our memories from the highlands of our imaginations. This process of bridging the gaps in our memories with things that may have been true is called *refabrication*. It is the process of building up a memory from bits and pieces of truth. Adding a fringe of untruth probably occurs in nearly all of our everyday reports of facts, not just reports of events that happened long ago. Once this occurs, the refabrication becomes a memory; it seems real and it is almost impossible to distinguish it from a real memory.

Donald Norman (Norman, 1970; Lindsay & Norman, 1972) has asked people such questions as "What were you doing 16 months ago?" or "What were you doing on Monday afternoon in the third week of September two years ago?" Here is a typical response to the second question:

1. Come on. How should I know? (Experimenter: Just try it, anyhow.)
2. OK, let's see: Two years ago. . . .
3. I would be in high school in Pittsburgh. . . .
4. That would be my senior year.
5. Third week in September—that's just after summer—that would be the fall term. . . .
6. Let me see. I think I had chemistry lab on Mondays.
7. I don't know. I was probably in the chemistry lab. . . .
8. Wait a minute—that would be the second week of school. I remember he started off with the atomic table—a big, fancy chart. I thought he was crazy, trying to make us memorize that thing.
9. You know, I think I can remember sitting. . . .

This response protocol illustrates how we may accomplish this type of retrieval problem. First we try to rephrase the question in the form of a specific date and then try to determine what we have been doing around that time. The search is organized around prominent temporal features, or "landmarks," in memory; these landmarks are used as starting points in the search (Line 3, "my senior year"). From the protocol, we can see that the process is not an easy one, and it certainly is not a case of simple recall. What we observe is fragmentary recall of what has in fact been experienced (Line 8, "a big fancy chart") with reconstructions of what must have been experienced (Line 9, "I think I can remember sitting . . .").

"At what time did you first leave home 5 days ago?" King and Pontious (1969) asked college students this question. Typically a student first recalled the time of his first class of the day, then recalled some event that occurred prior to leaving home, and then moved from that prior event to the time that he left home. Because the time of one's first class of the day is a highly discriminable event (getting to class on time occurs repeatedly—at least it should!), this experiment is another illustration of the use of landmarks as starting points for the recall of a desired event.

There is one serious problem with experiments that try to study refabrication by asking people questions about their past. How do we distinguish responses that come from the "lowlands of memory" from those that come from the "highlands of imagination"? To get around this problem, some investigators have provided a subject with an "experience" and then have tested his recall of that experience.

Empirical studies of the constructive process: Bartlett's "remembering".   During the 1920s and 1930s, in Cambridge, England, Sir Frederick Bartlett was performing his now classical studies of how people recall meaningful material. He reported his work in a book called *Remembering: A Study in Experimental and Social Psychology* (1932). In one series of experiments, Bartlett used the method of repeated reproduction: a subject studied a story or a drawing and was later asked repeatedly to reproduce the information. In another set of experiments, Bartlett used the method of serial reproduction: a complex story was read by one subject, who told it to another, who in turn told it to another, and so on (much as in the game of "telephone"). When Bartlett analyzed the results from either method, he observed that memory for even the simplest material was extremely inaccurate. The versions of a story became shorter, more concrete, and more modern in phraseology as it passed from person to person. This tendency was especially marked in the reproductions of Bartlett's story "The war of the ghosts." Here, the original sentence "One night two young men from Egulac went down to the river to hunt seals . . ." became after passing through the minds of a few subjects "Two Indians were out fishing. . . ." Most subjects were unaware that they were making these changes in the material. Bartlett commented on the large amount of construction he observed, and he proposed that memory was more a process of reconstruction than recollection. We do not remember some event by activating some fixed memory trace; instead we reconstruct the event—we build a *schema*, which is Bartlett's term for "an active organization of past reactions, or of past experiences."

Observation of live events. Some studies have gone beyond the technique of providing a story to remember; they have provided a seemingly true to life event to remember. In the early 1900s, for example, the following scene occurred in a Berlin classroom. Professor von Liszt, a famous criminologist, was speaking about a book, when suddenly a student shouted "I wanted to throw light on the matter from the standpoint of Christian morality!" A second student shouted "I cannot stand that!" The first student said "You have insulted me!" to which the second clenched his fist and cried out "If you say another word . . ." The first student pulled a gun out of his pocket, the second student rushed toward the first, the Professor stepped in to grasp the arm of the student with the gun, and the gun went off. The classroom became chaotic. At that point, the Professor calmed everyone down, and asked the students to write down exactly what they had observed.

The unannounced battle had been prearranged and carefully rehearsed for the purpose of studying recall (Muensterburg, 1908). Muensterburg observed the same things that Bartlett would observe some 20 years later: that the variations in the accounts of the incident were enormous. Many details were eliminated from witness's reports, and many "nonfacts" were added. The percentage of erroneous statements per witness ranged from 26 to 80, with recollections about the second half of the incident (the half that was more strongly "emotional") showing about 15% more mistakes than those of the first half. As Muensterburg (1908) put it:

> Words were put into the mouths of men who had been silent spectators during the whole short episode; actions were attributed to the chief participants of which not the slightest trace existed; and essential parts of the tragi-comedy were completely eliminated from the memory of a number of witnesses [pp. 50–51].

Variations of Professor von Liszt's dramatic demonstration have been carried out in psychology classrooms. The basic idea of having witnesses report on a staged event has also been used in a number of psychological experiments. For example, in one recent experiment (Buckhout, 1972, 1974) 141 people witnessed a student "attack" a professor; the incident was recorded on videotape so that it could be compared to eyewitness reports. After the incident, each witness gave a sworn statement in which he described the perpetrator of the crime, and all details that could be remembered about the incident. Most people could not describe the incident or any details very accurately. People tended to overestimate the passage of time, for example, by a factor of over two to one. The attacker's weight was estimated too high, and his age was underestimated. Seven weeks later, each witness was presented with a set of six photographs and only 40% identified the attacker correctly. Twenty-five percent of the witnesses identified as the culprit an innocent man who happened to be at the scene of the crime. In fact, even the professor who was attacked identified the innocent bystander. This example leads us to our next topic: eyewitness identification.

Eyewitness identification.   Mary Killean testified that on June 16, 1958, she was employed by National Tea Company at 3100 West Peterson, Chicago. Just before closing time a man with a gun informed her that it was a holdup, took $254 which she set on the counter, and left. Fred Capon was indicted some time later for armed robbery. He entered a plea of not guilty, was tried before a jury that found him guilty, and was sentenced to the penitentiary for a term of not less than 1 year nor more than life. Mary Killean's testimony reveals that she positively identified the defendant at the trial. The defendant's wife and a friend, Margaret Poston, testified that, at the time of the holdup, the defendant was with them in Indiana (People vs. Capon, 1961). Identification testimony was, in this case, the pivotal factor in determining the verdict. How much can we trust this type of evidence? An experiment at Dartmouth college on the accuracy of identification provides evidence bearing on this question (H. B. Brown, 1935). While a class was in session, a man dressed in workman's clothing entered the room, passed in front of the instructor's desk, tinkered with the radiator for a few minutes, made some remarks about the heat, and left the room. About 2 weeks later, the man returned to the classroom with five other workmen of the same general appearance. The six men lined up in front of the class, and the students were asked to indicate on a questionnaire which man they had seen earlier, and how confident they were about their judgment.

In one group of 64 unsuspecting sophomores, 11 or 17% could not make a correct identification; they picked out the wrong man. What is particularly interesting about this experiment, however concerns a group of students who had not witnessed the original incident but who were treated by the experimenter as though they had. These students were told they had witnessed an event about 2 weeks earlier and were asked to "identify" a man that they had actually never seen before. About 71% were correct in reporting that they did not remember the incident at all, but 29% "recalled" an incident they had never witnessed and tried to identify one of the men. Not only do the results of this experiment show the unreliability of identification testimony, but it demonstrates once again, the process of construction at work.

It is important to ask what goes on in a person's mind when he is trying to make a truthful report, but makes a false one. Possibly the person is lying, but more probably his false report is the result of normal constructive processes at work. At the time a person is asked to recall some complex event, he must retrieve information about that event from long-term store. Long-term store may contain some of the necessary information, but the information may be incomplete, especially if substantial time has elapsed between the original perception and its recall. To make up for the gaps in memory, the witness may unconsciously add bits and pieces to his recollection, even if those bits and pieces are not truly remembered. We shall return to the topic of constructive processes in eyewitness testimony in Chapter 8, where we consider ways in which leading questions can influence a witness's construction.

Constructive processes: A summary.   By now it should be clear that Walter De La Mare (Bartlett's *Familiar Quotations*) knew what he was talking about when he wrote the lines: "Memory—that strange deceiver! Who can trust her? How believe her—." Apparently what happens when we try to recall pictures, stories, or events from the past is that we remember an overall theme and then we construct the rest. We supply facts, largely unconsciously, to round out our knowledge. We infer from partial information. Contemporary models of memory (for example, Anderson & Bower, 1973; Rumelhart, Lindsay, & Norman, 1972) now explicitly embrace the active, constructive nature of recall.

SUMMARY

In Chapter 4, we introduced the topic of long-term memory and discussed ways in which material in long-term store is acquired, stored, and forgotten. In this chapter, we have gone one step further and considered some of the current work dealing with memory for material that has a good deal of meaning. We have found that when a person is presented with new meaningful material, he tends to remember the gist of that material but does not remember much about how the material was precisely worded. In addition, a person often remembers only parts of the newly learned material, and he tends to construct other bits and pieces in order to have a coherent story. That is, given that a few facts are remembered, other facts are constructed that are consistent with what is remembered. This process may occur without a person's awareness and illustrates the constructive aspects of memory for meaningful material.

7

Semantic Memory

Long-term memory contains what seems to be an infinite amount of information. It contains facts about our personal experiences, such as what we did on our last birthday, or, in rarer cases, what the first toy we ever had looked like (see Figure 7.1). Endel Tulving (1972) has used the term *episodic memory* to refer to our record of personal life experiences. In general, episodic memory contains any information the basis for retrieval of which is some association with a particular

FIGURE 7.1 Some examples of information in episodic memory.

time and/or place. For example, the information that "I learned the words 'hat,' 'picture,' and 'grandfather' in a psychology experiment today" is episodic information.

In contrast to episodic information, however, our memory also contains information that is not associated with a particular time or place, for example, the fact that a banana is yellow. The term *semantic memory* is used in reference to this nonepisodic information. Semantic memory includes the organized knowledge we have about words and other verbal symbols, their meaning, and referents; about relationships among them; and about rules for manipulating them. This chapter is about semantic memory. It is about the structure of the information contained in our semantic memory store and about the way in which we retrieve and use semantic information when we need it.

RETRIEVAL OF INFORMATION FROM SEMANTIC MEMORY

It has been pointed out in Chapter 4 that we are very good at reaching into our store of semantic information and producing a response that is appropriate to a question asked of us. In addition to quickly being able to find the answer to a question we have been asked before, we are also very good at producing a response to questions that we have never been asked before. Consider, for example, these questions:

1. Who was the first President of the United States?
2. What is the name of a Republican President?
3. What is the name of a fruit beginning with the letter P?

We do not have much trouble with these questions; in fact, most people can easily answer them within a few seconds. However, with all the information that we have stored, how do we do it? How do we manage to so quickly access the information necessary to answer these questions?

Successive scanning versus category access. To pose the question more specifically, we can ask whether the process of finding a desired item in semantic memory involves a "successive-scanning" process. *Successive scanning* here means to enter the memory store at some point or location and scan items one at a time until the sought-after information is found. If asked for the name of the first President of the United States, for example, we may go to the place in memory where "Presidents" are located and scan one by one until we find the one that is coded "first President." Hopefully, it is George Washington. If asked to name a fruit beginning with the letter P, we may go to our "fruits" and scan them one by one until we find one beginning with P. This is what we mean by successive scanning.

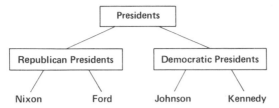

FIGURE 7.2   Hypothetical portion of semantic memory containing information about Presidents.

Alternatively, retrieval may not involve successive scanning of the contents of the memory store. As an example of what may be happening if we are not scanning successively, suppose again that you are asked for the name of a Republican President. You may go to the location in memory where "Presidents" are stored, and there you may find a subcategory of "Republican Presidents" as shown in Figure 7.2. You may enter the subcategory and pick the first item you find there. Although we are talking somewhat loosely the basic point is that information is retrieved by some process, and the question is: to what extent does the process involve successive scanning?

The Freedman–Loftus retrieval experiment.   To investigate these and related issues, Freedman and Loftus (1971) asked subjects to answer a large number of simple questions similar to the ones above. The specific purpose of the Freedman–Loftus experiment was to determine whether a subject finds an appropriate instance by successively scanning through instances of the category. If he does, then it ought to take longer to produce a member of a larger category than to produce a member of a smaller one. For example, a subject should take longer to name a fruit starting with P than to name a season starting with W (because in the former case, he would have more searching to do than in the latter case). The results of the experiment indicated that this was not the case. That is to say, subjects took no longer to name a member of a large category than a member of a small category. Freedman and Loftus conclude that people probably do not use a successive-scanning process to retrieve information from semantic memory.

What factors do influence retrieval speed? To answer this question, Freedman and Loftus presented stimuli to their subjects using one of two methods. In the first method, the letter was shown first, followed by a pause, and then the category. For example, the letter P was shown, followed soon afterwards by the category "fruits." The subject may respond with "peach," "pear," or "plum" among other possibilities. Reaction time was measured from the time "fruit" appeared until the subject made his response. With this "letter first" method of presentation, as soon as the category "fruit" is shown, the subject must do three things. First he must find the place in memory where information about "fruits" is stored; in other words, he must go to or "enter" his "fruits" in memory. Let us call the time needed for this step t_1. Next, the subject must retrieve the relevant information from the category; that is, he must find an instance of the "fruit" category that begins with the letter P. Let us call the time needed for this step t_2. Finally, the subject must produce a response. We refer to the time needed to do this as k. The total reaction time (RT_1) to respond when given the stimulus "P–fruit" is therefore

$$RT_1 = t_1 + t_2 + k.$$

For half of the questions asked of any subject, the second method of presentation has been used: the category was presented before the letter. In the example we have been discussing, "fruit" was presented, followed by a pause, and then the letter P. Reaction time in this case was taken from presentation of P until a response was made. With this "category first" method of presentation, it is possible for the subject to go to or enter the category during the interval between "fruit" and P. Therefore, the time t_1 is not included in the total measured reaction time, and the reaction time in this case is

$$RT_2 = t_2 + k.$$

By subtracting RT_2 from RT_1 we can get an estimate of the duration of t_1, the time needed to enter the category (see Figure 7.3). In typical experiments, t_1 turns out to be about 250 milliseconds, or a quarter of a second. We can therefore see that there is fairly good evidence for a two-step theory of retrieval. When we discuss various theories of semantic memory, we shall see that all of them involve two retrieval stages of one sort or another.

How does one retrieval affect another?   Several experiments have been conducted on the issue of how one retrieval from memory affects another. Collins and Quillian (1970), for example, have presented such sentences as "A canary is a bird" and required their subjects to decide whether the sentences were true or false. Prior exposure to one sentence, they have found, reduces the reaction time to a second sentence, sometimes by over a half a second, whenever the same subject

Condition 1:

"p" – interval – "Fruit" |____ RT_1 ____| Response (e.g., "Pear")

$RT_1 = t_1$ (enter fruits)

    $+ t_2$ (find a fruit beginning with P)

    $+ k$ (respond)

Condition 2:

"Fruit" – interval – "p" |____ RT_2 ____| Response (e.g., "Pear")

$RT_2 = t_2$ (find a fruit beginning with P)

    $+ k$ (respond)

FIGURE 7.3   Reaction time taken to produce a fruit beginning with the letter P depends on whether "FRUIT" or "P" is presented first.

noun has been used. To illustrate, prior exposure to "A canary is a bird" reduced the time subjects took to verify other sentences about canaries.

Facilitation has also been observed in experiments in which a subject must name a member of a category, and some time later must name a different member of the category (cf. E. F. Loftus, 1973a; Loftus & Loftus, 1974b). Try this: what is the name of a fruit beginning with the letter A? Now, what is the name of a fruit beginning with P? People usually answer the second question much more easily if it has been preceded by the first one. Why should this be?

One possible explanation is that the first retrieval of a "fruit" increases the accessibility or "activates" one or more memory locations, making information retrieval from them easier when the second retrieval is made. For example, presentation of the category "fruit" may activate the memory location representing the category name itself, and it may, in addition, activate the locations that are nearby the location of the category name. If we add the plausible assumption that this greater accessibility of the memory location(s) is temporary and decays gradually (after all, things cannot stay activated forever), then we can make one additional prediction: as we increase the time, or the number of different unrelated questions, that intervene between our two critical questions, we should reduce the facilitating effect. Figure 7.4 shows that this is exactly what has been observed in an experiment in which subjects have had to produce a member of a category and, after zero, one, or two intervening retrievals, have had to produce a different

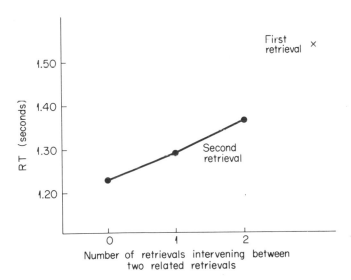

FIGURE 7.4   Results of the Loftus (1973a) experiment. Mean reaction time to a second retrieval as a function of the number of retrievals that intervene between that second retrieval and an earlier related retrieval. The × refers to the time taken to produce a category member when no other members of the category have been previously produced. (After Loftus, 1973a.)

member of the category. The time to produce an initial category member (for example, a fruit beginning with P when no other fruits had been retrieved earlier) was 1.52 seconds. However, a subject was able to produce a "fruit–P" in 1.21 seconds if he had named a different fruit on the previous trial; in 1.29 seconds if he had named a different fruit two trials back, and in 1.38 seconds if he had named a different fruit three trials back. The data in Figure 7.4 clearly demonstrate that if we ask a subject to name a member of a category and soon afterward ask him to name a different member of the category, facilitation occurs and this facilitation declines as we increase the number of items intervening between the two critical retrievals. It appears as if memory locations can become activated temporarily.

Relationship between semantic memory structure and retrieval: A problem for theories. Before we get into theories of semantic memory we should point out a serious limitation inherent in such theories: in order to theorize about a *retrieval* process, we need to know something about the *structure* from which we are retrieving. An analogy will make this point clearer. In order to retrieve a book from the New York Public Library we have to know something about how the books are arranged or structured in the library. We may have a good deal of information about the book we want; for example, that it is called *Human Information Processing*, that it has been written by Lindsay and Norman, that it has a yellow cover, and that it is over 700 pages long. However, unless we know something about how the Public Library is structured, and specifically where psychology books are kept, we may spend a month looking for the book and still never find it.

Returning to the issue of semantic memory, any theory of *retrieval from semantic memory* must, then, also postulate a *structure of semantic memory*. Structure and retrieval are inextricably entwined. This places an inherent limitation on the extent to which an experiment can be used to test either the retrieval or the structural aspect of some theory, because if an experiment does not support the theory, there is no way to know which aspect of the theory is at fault. Is it the structure or the retrieval process that should be revised? We shall now turn to some models of semantic memory and see how this problem has been handled.

MODELS OF SEMANTIC MEMORY

For purposes of this discussion we shall follow the lead of Smith, Shoben, and Rips (1974) and make a distinction between three types of semantic memory models: network models, set-theoretic models, and feature-comparison models.

Network models. In 1969, Allan Collins and Ross Quillian wrote a paper entitled "Retrieval time from semantic memory." In this paper, Collins and Quillian suggest that the items stored in semantic memory are connected by links in a huge network. Figure 7.5 presents a portion of this hypothetical memory

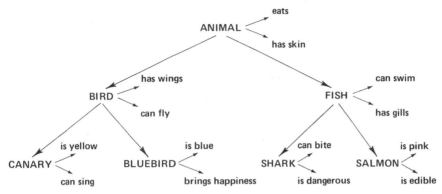

FIGURE 7.5   A portion of a hierarchically organized memory structure. (After Collins & Quillian, 1969.)

structure. Notice that the concepts in this structure are hierarchically organized into logically nested subordinate–superordinate relations. For example, the superordinate of CANARY is BIRD, and the superordinate of BIRD is ANIMAL. Notice further that a property characterizing a particular class of things is assumed to be stored only at the place in the hierarchy that corresponds to that class. This assumption has been called the assumption of "cognitive economy." For example, a property that characterizes all birds (such as the fact that they have wings) is stored only at BIRD. It is not stored again with the different types of birds, even though other types of birds also have wings.

Given this hypothesized network structure, Collins and Quillian's next task was to determine how information is retrieved from the structure. To answer this question, an experiment was carried out in which subjects were asked to answer "Yes" or "No" to simple questions. Consider, for example, the following questions about canaries:

1.   Does a canary eat?
2.   Does a canary fly?
3.   Is a canary yellow?

Referring back to the hypothesized structure (Figure 7.3) the three questions above may be characterized by the *semantic level* at which the information needed to answer them is stored. Consider the first question, "Does a canary eat?" The information "eats" is stored with ANIMAL two levels away from CANARY. Likewise, the information "has wings" and "is yellow" (needed to answer the second and third questions) is stored one and zero levels away from CANARY, respectively. The major data of interest in Collins and Quillian's experiment were the *reaction time* to respond to the questions. (Naturally, questions such as those above were intermixed with such other questions as "Does a canary have gills?" for which the correct answer is "No.")

The results of the experiment are shown in Figure 7.6. With increasing level of information, it takes increasing amounts of time to retrieve it. Collins and Quillian explain these data as follows: in order to answer Question 3, the subject must first enter the level in memory that corresponds to CANARY and here quickly finds the information that canaries are yellow. The question is therefore answered relatively fast. To answer the second question ("Does a canary fly?") the subject still enters memory at CANARY but does not find any information at that level concerning whether or not canaries fly. Because a canary is a bird, however, the subject moves up the hierarchy to the level where information about birds is stored and then finds that birds fly. Combining the information that canaries are birds and birds fly, the question can then be answered. Because of the extra step of moving up the hierarchy Question 2 takes somewhat longer to answer than Question 3. Question 1 ("Does a canary eat?") takes even longer for the same sort of reason. To answer Question 1, the subject cannot use any of the information that is stored at either CANARY or BIRD but must move up to an additional level in the hierarchy to ANIMAL. Because a canary is a bird, and a bird is an animal, and animals eat, it is concluded that a canary must eat too. Therefore, the reason some questions take longer to answer than others is that some questions require more traveling from level to level in the semantic hierarchy. Using a similar rationale, Collins and Quillian predict that it takes less time to answer "Is a canary a bird?" than to answer "Is a canary an animal?" Referring back to Figure 7.5 we see that to answer the latter question, a subject must move up two levels from CANARY to ANIMAL, whereas to answer the former question, the subject must move up only one level.

A closer inspection of Figure 7.6 reveals that on the average, people take about 75 milliseconds longer to answer the question "Does a canary eat?" than to

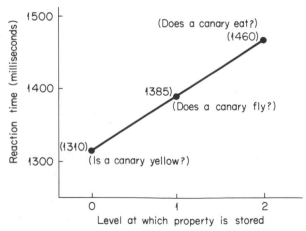

FIGURE 7.6   Reaction time taken to answer questions about various nouns and their properties. (After Collins & Quillian, 1969.)

answer "Does a canary fly?" and about 75 milliseconds longer to answer the question about flying than to answer "Is a canary yellow?" Within the context of Collins and Quillian's model, therefore, the time necessary to travel from one level of the hierarchy to the next level is about 75 milliseconds.

Other network models.   Before we discuss some problems with Collins and Quillian's approach, we briefly mention some of the other major efforts in this domain. Elaborate network models have been proposed by Anderson and Bower (1973), by Rumelhart, Lindsay, and Norman (1972), by Kintsch (1972, 1974), and by Loftus (1973b). As we have pointed out above, network models conceive of semantic memory as a giant network of interconnected nodes. The nodes usually correspond to individual concepts, ideas, or events in the system. The links or connections between the nodes specify particular relations that hold between the concepts. To illustrate, the system may have the concepts DOG and ANIMAL, which may be represented as distinct nodes with a connection between them specifying that a dog is a member of or a subset of ANIMAL.

To date, Anderson and Bower have one of the most elaborate models, a description of which fills a 524 page book called *Human Associative Memory*, better known as HAM. Rumelhart, Lindsay, and Norman call their model ELINOR (possibly a merging if the three names of ELINOR's creators?). Unlike Collins and Quillian's model, both HAM and ELINOR have the capacity to "learn" new material. The Kintsch and Loftus models, in contrast, are more concerned with semantic organization and retrieval mechanisms. Because Collins and Quillian's original model is somewhat simpler than the others and has been around somewhat longer, it has received massive attention (both friendly and hostile) in the literature of semantic memory.

Problems with the Collins and Quillian model.   Most college students know what a mammal is, and if we add this concept to a hypothetical network that contains COLLIE, DOG, and ANIMAL, it is placed between DOG and ANI-MAL. In a semantic hierarchy, MAMMAL is closer than ANIMAL to either DOG or to some particular type of dog (for example, COLLIE). According to Collins and Quillian's model, a person should answer the question "Is a collie a mammal?" faster than the question "Is a collie an animal?" However, people don't (Rips, Shoben, & Smith, 1973). Similarly, people take longer to answer "Is a cantaloupe a melon?" than to answer "Is a cantaloupe a fruit?" even though melon is logically closer to cantaloupe in a semantic hierarchy (Rips, Shoben, & Smith, 1973). Findings such as these cause trouble for Collins and Quillian. One way around this problem is to eliminate the requirement that some nodes are intermediate between others and to allow for the possibility that all concepts are connected directly to all other concepts. COLLIE may then be "farther" from MAMMAL than from ANIMAL (possibly because it is a less frequent associate).

The cognitive economy assumption—that a property which characterizes a particular class of things is stored only at the place in the hierarchy that corresponds to that class—has also been questioned. Anderson and Bower (1973, p. 381) state their objection: "There is no compelling reason to believe that human memory cannot retain any redundant facts; there is no strong need for erasure or garbage collection of redundant facts just to 'clean up' the memory system."

C. Conrad (1972), meanwhile, attacked the cognitive economy assumption on experimental grounds. Conrad simply asked subjects to describe a canary, a bird, an animal, and so on. She then tabulated the frequency with which various properties were mentioned. It turned out that the properties frequently associated with canary (such as the fact that they are yellow) were the properties presumed by Collins and Quillian to be stored directly at the CANARY node, whereas the properties that Conrad found to be less frequent were presumed by Collins and Quillian to be stored with BIRD or with ANIMAL. It may very well be, therefore, that property frequency rather than the hierarchical distance determines retrieval time. In fact, in an experiment to test for this possibility, C. Conrad has found that property frequency has a large effect on reaction time, whereas hierarchical distance does not.

Parenthetically, we should note that Conrad's disconfirmation of the cognitive economy assumption illustrates the danger of taking a physical analogy too seriously. In Chapter 1, we have pointed out that the information-processing approach derives in large part from a computer analogy. For computers, space economy is critical because computers have a limited memory capacity. However, computers process information very fast. A computer analogy therefore suggests economy of space (that is, cognitive economy) at the expense of additional processing (that is, having to move up and down a hierarchy to find needed information). However, humans are probably somewhat different; they process information relatively slowly but appear to have virtually infinite storage capacity. So humans can probably operate more efficiently by storing information very redundantly and thereby cutting down on the processing time necessary to find the information. Allan Collins and Ross Quillian are expert computer programmers as well as scientists, and probably this is why the cognitive economy assumption suggested itself to them.

Set-theoretic models.   Whereas network models have emphasized the netlike hierarchical structure of semantic memory, a different class of models, called *set-theoretic models*, has treated memory as if it consists of sets of elements. The elements in a particular set may be all the exemplars of that set. So one set may include all instances of dogs, whereas another set may include all instances of fruits. The elements in a set may also include attributes of the concept represented by that set. So one set may include all the attributes of DOG (for example, that it bites, barks, wags its tail), whereas another set might include all attributes of FRUIT (that it is edible, has seeds, is sweet).

We shall use as an example of a set-theoretic model one proposed by David Meyer (1970). Meyer's "attribute" model assumes that memory consists of sets of attributes. For example, COLLIE would be represented by a set of the defining attributes of a collie, and DOG would be similarly represented by a set of the defining attributes of a dog. The process of answering a question such as "Is a collie a dog?" is then thought to involve a decision as to whether every attribute included in DOG is also an attribute included in COLLIE.

This process of comparing attributes actually forms the second stage of a two-stage model proposed by Meyer (1970). In order to understand the model, we need to consider Meyer's research in more detail. A subject in Meyer's experiment underwent a procedure illustrated in Figure 7.7. On a display screen in front of the subject, a sentence frame such as "All ____ are ____" (in one condition) or "Some ____ are ____" (in another condition) appeared. The blank spaces were then filled with the names of two semantic categories, which are referred to as S and P. For example, S could be collies and P could be dogs, resulting in the statement "All collies are dogs" or "Some collies are dogs." The subject's job was to indicate whether the statement was true or false by pressing one of two keys. Meyer found that statements using the word "some" led to faster responses than statements using the word "all." Why should this be?

To account for this fact and some of the other more complex observed results, Meyer's model involves a two-stage process. For statements using the word "all," the subject first retrieves the set of all categories that have some members in common, or intersect, with the P category ("dog" in the above example.) If the S category ("collie" in this case) intersects the P category, the second stage of the process is executed: the subject decides whether every attribute of the P category is also an attribute of the S category. To decide if "all collies are dogs," therefore, the subject first determines that the two categories do intersect and then determines that every attribute of DOG is also an attribute of COLLIE.

For statements involving the word "some," only Stage 1 (deciding whether S and P intersect) is needed. To decide that "some females are professors,"

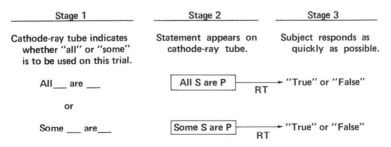

FIGURE 7.7   Display sequence on a typical trial during an experiment by Meyer (1970).

the subject only needs to decide that FEMALES and PROFESSORS intersect (that is, only one example is needed). It is therefore clear why the model predicts that "some" statements should be verified more quickly than "all" statements: "some" statements require one stage to be executed, whereas "all" statements require two.

It is clear why this type of model is called a set-theoretic model. For each item in memory, the model assumes that there are two sets of interest: (1) the set of categories that *intersect* with the item and (2) the set of attributes that *define* the item.

Problems with set-theoretic models.   To appreciate one of the major difficulties with set-theoretic models, consider Lakoff's (1972) analysis of "hedges." Hedges are linguistic modifiers that are used to qualify statements that we make about things. "Technically speaking" is a hedge and can be used in the sentence, "Technically speaking a chicken is a bird." "Loosely speaking a bat is a bird" is another sentence showing a hedge in action, and it means something such as "A bat is kind of like a bird, but it's not really a bird." A set model has difficulty explaining our use of such hedges. There is no intersection between the categories "bat" and "bird" (that is, no bats are really birds) so how can a person using a model such as Meyer's ever correctly verify such hedged statements as the one about bats? Considerations such as these have led Smith, Shoben, and Rips (1974) to propose a feature-comparison model, which we discuss in the next section.

The   Smith,   Shoben,   and   Rips   feature-comparison   model. Following the lead of Katz and Fodor (1963), Smith *et al.* (1974) begin with the assumption that the meaning of any item in memory can be represented as a set of semantic features. In this sense the model resembles a set-theoretic model, but Smith and his colleagues have made a critical new assumption: that there are two distinct types of features. First, there are those features which are essential aspects of the item's meaning. These are known as *defining features.* Conversely, other features do not form part of the item's definition, but are nonetheless descriptive of the item. These are referred to as *characteristic features.* To illustrate these two kinds of features, consider the word *robin.* There are some features that must be true of robins, such as they are "living," "have feathers," "have wings," and "have red breasts." These are defining features. Other features, however, may be associated with robins, but they are not necessary to define a robin. These include features such as "like to perch in trees," "undomesticated," "harmless," and "smallish." In situations where a subject must decide whether an instance is a member of a category (for example, deciding whether a robin is a bird), it is assumed that the sets of features corresponding to the instance and the category are partitioned into the two subsets corresponding to defining and characteristic features. Figure 7.8 illustrates this partitioning for ROBIN and for BIRD.

Concepts

	Robin	Bird
Defining features	Is living Has feathers Has wings Has a red breast . . .	Is living Has feathers Has wings . . .
Characteristic features	Flys Pearches in trees Is undomesticated Is smallish . . .	Flys . .

FIGURE 7.8   The meaning of a concept is defined in terms of semantic features. The higher on the list a feature is, the more essential it is for defining the concept. (After Smith *et al.*, 1974. Copyright 1974 by the American Psychological Association. Reproduced by permission.)

The process of verifying whether an instance is a member of a category (in this case, is a robin a bird?) is now assumed to be accomplished in two major stages that are schematized in the flow chart of Figure 7.9. The first stage involves a comparison of *both* the defining and the characteristic features of the instance and the category to determine the degree to which the two sets of features are similar. If there is a high degree of correspondence between the instance features and the category features, the subject responds "Yes" immediately. If the two sets of features have very little correspondence (low similarity), the subject can respond "No" immediately. If, however, there is an intermediate level of similarity between the features of the instance and the features of the category, then a second stage is needed before the subject can reach a decision. In the second stage, the subject compares only the defining features of the instance and the category. If all the defining features of the category are also defining features of the instance, then a "Yes" response is made; otherwise the subject responds "No." This aspect of the model is much the same as Stage 2 of Meyer's model, discussed above. (See Smith *et al.*, 1974, for an extended description of the feature-comparison model.)

How well does this model describe the findings in the semantic memory literature? We consider three results, the first of which is called the *typicality effect*. When a subject is asked to verify whether an instance is a member of a category, say BIRDS, subjects are consistently faster in verifying some instances (for example, ROBIN, CANARY) than others (for example, CHICKEN). The faster instances are those that are judged by other, independent subjects to be more typical of the category. The typicality effect has been observed in at least three different laboratories (Rips, Shoben, & Smith, 1973; Rosch, 1973; Wilkins, 1971). The feature-comparison model explains this result by assuming that if the instance to be verified is highly typical of the

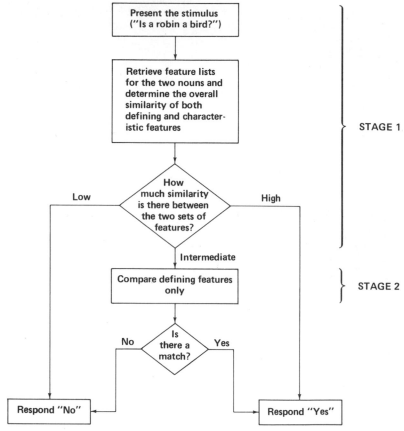

FIGURE 7.9   The Feature Comparison Model for the verification of such statements as "Is a robin a bird?" (After Smith *et al.*, 1974.)

category, the two share a large number of features (both defining and characteristic). When it is discovered during Stage 1 that the instance and category have largely overlapping features, the subject can make an immediate response without executing Stage 2. For atypical instances, in contrast, there is not much overlap in terms of the characteristic features. Stage 2 must therefore be executed, and response time is accordingly longer. To summarize the argument, the reason typical instances are verified faster than atypical ones is that the typical instances may require only Stage 1, whereas the atypical ones often require both Stages 1 and 2.

Consider now the finding of Collins and Quillian (1969) that people take longer to verify that a canary is an animal than they take to verify that a canary is a bird. Again, this result may be explained simply by assuming that the features of CANARY overlap more with those of its immediate superordinate, BIRD, than with those of its less immediate superordinate, ANIMAL. In the former case, then, Stage 2 processing is more likely to be omitted. It is interesting to observe what happens when a concept is *less* similar to its immediate superordinate than it is to its less immediate superordinate. This is the case involving (according to typicality ratings) DOG, which is less similar to MAMMAL than it is to ANIMAL. As noted above, subjects take longer to verify that a dog is a mammal than they take to verify that a dog is an animal.

Finally, how does the model handle the hedges that we have discussed above? How is it that we are able to say "Loosely speaking, a bat is a bird," whereas we would not make the flat statement, "A bat is a bird."? According to Smith *et al.* (1974), the phrase "loosely speaking" indicates that the instance in question (in this case, a bat) possesses many of the characteristic features of the category (in this case, of birds). However, it is not the case that all the defining features of the category are also defining features of the instance. When confronted with "Loosely speaking, a bat is a bird" the proposed two-stage retrieval process does two things: (1) in Stage 1, it determines that bats and birds do possess many features in common and (2) in Stage 2, it determines that bats do not possess all the defining features of birds. Although it may therefore be reasonable to say "Loosely speaking, a bat is a bird" because many characteristic features are present, a knowledgeable person does not say "A bat is a bird" because Stage 2 processing determines that the defining features of the two concepts do not completely match. However, under time pressure in reaction time experiments, subjects do sometimes erroneously respond "Yes" to "Is a bat a bird?" This is expected by the feature-comparison model, because it predicts that subjects occasionally omit Stage 2 and make a fast "Yes" response on the basis of the large overall number of overlapping features between "bat" and "bird."

The second hedge we discuss above is "technically speaking"; for example, "Technically speaking, a chicken is a bird." This hedge is also handled elegantly by the model, which simply assumes that "technically speaking" is used for an instance that has the defining features but not very many characteristic features of some category. A chicken, for example, is indeed a bird, because it does have the defining features (that is, it has wings, lays eggs, has a beak). However, a chicken doesn't have the characteristic features of a bird—it doesn't sing, it doesn't fly, it's too large, etc. So it's only "technically" a bird.

Problems with the feature-comparison model.   As appealing as the feature-comparison model is, at least two problems with it are evident. The first problem, pointed out by Collins and Loftus (1975), is that the distinction between defining and characteristic features has the inherent difficulty that there is no feature that is absolutely necessary to define something. For example, if a person removes the wings from a bird, that object does not cease to be a bird. If the feathers are plucked from a robin, it does not stop being a robin. Furthermore, people do not appear to be able to make consistent decisions as to whether a feature is defining or characteristic. Is "having four legs" a defining feature of tables? What if you see a tablelike object with only three legs? Do you still call it a table? Smith and his co-workers appear to have recognized that features are more or less defining, but they have been forced into making what is probably a somewhat artificial distinction between defining and characteristic features.

A second problem with the feature comparison model is that it cannot explain a result observed by Glass and Holyoak (1975). To better appreciate this failure of the model, consider the process of deciding that something is not something else (for example, "Is a banana a robin?"). In this example, the two nouns, "banana" and "robin," have almost zero features in common, and a subject should therefore say "No" very quickly. However, what about the question "Is a collie a robin?" It should take somewhat longer, because the subject may determine that the two nouns have some features in common (for example, both are living) and therefore execute Stage 2. The feature-comparison model thus expects that the more related two nouns are, the longer it takes the subject to say "No." Glass and Holyoak (1975) have investigated the speed with which subjects can disconfirm various types of false statements. The result that is damaging for the feature-comparison model is that subjects can disconfirm a false statement such as "Some chairs are tables" faster than a statement such as "Some chairs are rocks," even though chairs and tables are more similar to each other than chairs and rocks.

SEMANTIC MEMORY: A FINAL COMMENT

Most laboratory experiments of human memory have dealt with episodic memory phenomena; many fewer have dealt with semantic memory phenomena. We have sampled a little of the vast literature on episodic memory in Chapters 4 and 6 and a little of the somewhat scantier literature on semantic memory in this chapter. It is certainly the case that many more experimental and theoretical developments are needed for a full understanding of how the semantic store is organized and how information from it is retrieved.

Another important problem for students of memory is to determine the interdependence between episodic and semantic memory. Suppose, for example, you witness an automobile accident, which is a highly complex and sudden event often lasting only a few seconds. The knowledge contained in semantic memory influences your perception and memory for this event.

A recent experiment (E. Loftus & Zanni, 1975) demonstrated this quite clearly: college students watched films of traffic accidents and then answered questions about events occurring in the film. Some of the students were asked questions containing an indefinite article (for example, ''Did you see a broken headlight?''), whereas other students were asked questions containing a definite article (for example, ''Did you see the broken headlight?''). In fact, there was no broken headlight in the film. Questions containing a definite article produced many more ''Yes'' responses, indicating ''false'' recognition of events that never in fact occurred.

Why does this happen? Apparently, when asked ''Did you see *the* . . . ?'' a person familiar with the semantic rules governing the use of the ''the'' (a part of semantic memory) is likely to infer that the object has, in fact, been present. After all, we use the definite article when we are referring to a particular object, and we use the indefinite ''a'' when we refer to any member of a class of objects. Conversely, the indefinite article is not likely to lead to the inference that the object has been present. This effect illustrates something very important, namely, that a person's semantic knowledge (in this case, his knowledge about the use of ''the'' and ''a'') can influence his report of an event he has experienced (in this case, an accident he has witnessed). The indication is that semantic memory and episodic memory depend highly on each other.

SUMMARY

The distinction between two types of long-term memories was initially proposed by Endel Tulving; ''episodic memory'' was the term he reserved to refer to memory for our personal experiences and their temporal relations, whereas ''semantic memory'' referred to our knowledge of words, concepts, and relations among the two. The material in this chapter dealt primarily with semantic memory. Investigators of human semantic memory are concerned with this question: how is this type of information structured in memory, and how do we retrieve it? To answer this very important question, experiments are usually conducted in which subjects are observed and sometimes timed while they retrieve very simple information. The data are used to make inferences about storage and retrieval processes, and several types of models have been proposed to account for these data. Network models, set-theoretic models, and the feature-comparison model are three that we have discussed.

8
Practical Applications

In the previous seven chapters, we have reviewed a theoretical framework that views man as an information-processing system and we have presented much of the basic research that serves to flesh out this framework. Now that we have the framework, we arrive at the questions: What good is it? What exactly can we do with it? In this chapter, we shall describe some of the practical, technological problems to which the theory and the research may be applied. Because the framework is still relatively new, much of its potential for practical application has yet to be realized. Therefore, in addition to describing practical applications that already exist, we shall not hesitate to speculate about what we consider to be potential future applications. We shall briefly describe four areas in which the information-processing view of man may prove profitable: those of mental diagnosis, of education, of human engineering, and of law.

COGNITIVE TASKS AS DIAGNOSTIC TESTS

For one reason or another, it is often desirable to assess the state of a person's mental functioning. The administration of an IQ test, for example, is a technique for measuring the efficacy of a person's intellectual abilities. The results of the IQ test can then provide the person with information about what skills he may be good at and what other skills he may be not so good at. Likewise, if a person sustains brain damage for some reason, tests can be administered to determine what aspects of mental functioning have been impaired. Information from these tests can then provide a guide for the sort of rehabilitation program that is best suited for the person. In a somewhat different realm, a person ingesting some drug or a counselor interested in drug abuse may want to learn which mental processes are altered by the effects of the drug.

Given the need for some specification of mental functioning, what form should such a specification take? We have argued that a human can be viewed as an information-processing system, and previous chapters of this book have identified various components of this system. To each such component, it is possible to assign a *value* that in some way reflects how efficient or inefficient the component is. We can speak, for example, of the *rate* of pattern recognition; of the *capacity* of short-term store; of the *rate* of short-term–long-term information transfer; of the *time* to retrieve information from long-term store, and so on.

These values can be measured using various cognitive tasks, or paradigms, which have evolved along with the construction of the system. As examples, Sperling's partial report and visual-scanning techniques allow measurement of the capacity of iconic store and the rate of pattern recognition (Chapter 2). The Brown–Peterson paradigm measures the rate of forgetting from short-term store; a memory-span procedure measures the capacity of short-term store; and Sternberg's scanning paradigm measures the speed of searching through short-term store (Chapter 3). The Hebb, Hellyer, and Rundus procedures provide an indication of how much information can be transferred to long-term store via rote rehearsal; the category clustering and organizational measures designed by Bousfield, Mandler, Tulving, and others allow us to specify how efficient a person is at encoding material for subsequent retrieval (Chapter 4). The Bransford–Franks task provides a possible measure of how a person integrates temporally separated verbal information (Chapter 6). Semantic memory procedures designed by Collins and Quillian, Loftus, and others measure how fast semantic information can be retrieved (Chapter 7).

These tasks and the theoretical structure within which to interpret them provide the potential wherewithal to allow a fairly precise specification of a person's cognitive processes, that is, his mental functioning. In this section we shall describe some of the research that has been done using cognitive tasks in diagnostic ways.

Individual differences.   In most situations that require diagnostic tests, we are interested in the functioning of an individual person and in how the functioning of that individual differs from the functioning of other individuals. The most common such situation involves the measurement of a person's intelligence quotient, or IQ.

Currently used IQ tests are descriptive and predictive. They are descriptive in the sense that performance on some IQ subtest is thought to describe a person's ability or skill in some given area. For example, performance on a quantitative subtest is thought to describe a person's ability to perform quantitative tasks in general. IQ tests are predictive in the sense that an individual's performance on an IQ test is correlated with his subsequent performance in some area of interest (for example, school grades).

The problem with IQ tests is that they provide very little information about *why* an individual is good or poor in some particular area. For instance, one may conclude from a person's score on the quantitative subtest that the person is poor at quantitative skills and therefore probably should not be an accountant or a statistician. However, the test in no way indicates which specific mental processes are responsible for the person's being poor at quantitative skills. This deficit of IQ tests is nicely summarized in an article by Earl Hunt and Marcy Lansman (1975):

> . . . consider an analogy [between the measurement of IQ and] the measurement of automobile abilities. An observer could develop a classificatory scheme by noting that vehicles differed in their weight, speed, gasoline consumption, turning ratio, and so forth. By appropriate statistical analyses, these data could be reduced to a small number of inferred dimensions. For instance, it would soon be noticed that weight, acceleration, and gasoline consumption covaried, and such an observation might lead to the derivation of an abstract concept of *power*. Certainly such a concept is useful in thinking about automobiles [just as the concept of, say, quantitative ability is useful in thinking about humans], but for a really adequate description of how a car works we use our knowledge of engine design, and of the workings of steering and transmission systems. A listing of vehicle characteristics just is not an adequate way to explain how an automobile negotiates a turn—or fails to.
>
> We find equally unsatisfactory the statement that an individual is or is not suited for a particular position "because of his or her IQ." In order to understand differences in intellectual performance we must know how performance occurs, and how specific individuals differ from the norm [pp. 81–82].

Hunt and his associates at the University of Washington have attacked the problem head on, with a project aimed at developing a new kind of "IQ test" that is based on an individual's performance in various cognitive tasks (Hunt, Frost, & Lunneborg, 1973; Hunt & Love, 1972; Hunt, Lunneborg, & Lewis, 1975; Hunt & Lansman, 1975). As a start, Hunt's research has focused on determining which components of the information-processing system are responsible for what are now termed "verbal and quantitative abilities." The research strategy involves the following. In Washington state, all high-school students take a form of IQ test (specifically, a scholastic aptitude test) as part of their college entrance requirements. This test provides measures of verbal and quantitative abilities. Students with various combinations of these abilities are then given a battery of cognitive tests and the question is: what correlates with what? Some interesting results have emerged, for example:

1. In one task, students with high as opposed to low quantitative ability were given paired-associate items to remember. Analysis of the results within the context of the Atkinson–Shiffrin memory model revealed that students with high quantitative ability maintained more information in short-term store and relied less heavily on storing information in long-term store than did low-quantitative students.

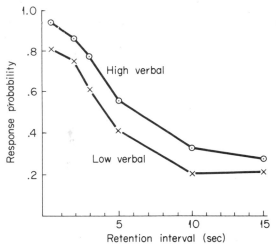

FIGURE 8.1   Low verbal subjects show faster forgetting and/or less initial long-term information in the Brown–Peterson task. (Adapted from Hunt, *et al.,* 1975.)

2. High-verbal students are able to search more rapidly through short-term store and have larger short-term store capacity than do low-verbal students in a Sternberg scanning paradigm.

3. In a Brown–Peterson short-term memory paradigm, high-verbal subjects show fewer errors at all retention intervals, as shown in Figure 8.1. This result indicates that low-verbal subjects forget faster from short-term store and/or that high-verbal subjects initially store more information in long-term store.

4. In an experiment designed by Bruner (reported in Hunt *et al.,* 1975) a new paradigm has been developed to measure an individual's ability to integrate verbal information over time. This paradigm involves presentation of nonsense syllables in a free-recall task. There are two types of lists: "word" lists contain adjacent pairs of syllables that when put together form a word. For example, two adjacent syllables in a word list may contain PROB as one syllable, followed by LEM as the next syllable. Control lists do not have such related syllables. The results of this experiment are shown in Table 8.1. High- and low-verbal subjects do not differ substantially on the control lists. However, high-verbal subjects are able to take advantage of the word lists considerably more than are the low-verbal subjects.

In a separate study (reported by Hunt & Lansman, 1975) a group of extremely good memorizers (mnemonists) were tested in an experiment that measured the rate of acquiring new information and also the rate of forgetting information from long-term store. The mnemonists showed faster and more efficient initial learning than did normal subjects, but normal subjects and mnemonists did not differ in terms of how fast they forgot.

TABLE 8.1

Low-Verbal Subjects Are Less Able to Take Advantage of
Inherent Semantic Structure Than Are High-Verbal Subjects.[a,b]

		Type of Subject	
		High-Verbal	Low-Verbal
Type of list	Words	.30	.15
	Nonsense syllables	.12	.11

[a] Numbers represent proportion of correct responses in the various conditions.

[b] Adapted from Hunt et. al. (1975).

In general, these and other results indicate that high-verbal individuals are able to manipulate information in short-term store considerably faster than are low-verbal individuals. Additionally, high-verbal people seem more adept at generating durable long-term memory codes. These results, however, are still somewhat preliminary. The end product of Hunt's research is hoped to be a new concept of intelligence, in which an individual's mental ability is specified by a list of scores on specific information-processing abilities. The existence of such a test is likely to lead to additional, practically oriented research within the context of the information-processing system we have been discussing. A crucial question is, what aspects of the information-processing system are modifiable by training? Can we, for example, teach a person to increase his rate of searching through short-term store? Moreover, given that some aspects of the system are modifiable, what skills can then be acquired by the person? For example, by speeding up short-term search rate are we changing a low-verbal person into a high-verbal person? The answers to these and related questions will be extremely valuable in terms of such things as being able to tailor abilities to jobs and vice versa.

Diagnosis of mental impairment.   The sorts of tasks used by Hunt in his quest for intelligence can also be used in diagnosing the specific deficits of individuals whose mental functioning is impaired. Such individuals include those who have had brain damage resulting from injury or sickness, as well as those who have been retarded from birth (for example, Down's syndrome or "mongoloid" individuals). Research by Baddeley and Warrington (1970) on the application of cognitive tasks to amnesic patients has already been discussed (Chapter 3). In general, it is relatively easy using a series of cognitive tasks to pinpoint where in the victim's information-processing system difficulty is occurring. Does the problem lie in overly rapid forgetting from short-term store? In an inability to transfer information to long-term store? Is there difficulty in retrieving information from semantic memory? Such information about the specific locus of deficits is useful in terms of (1) determining what sorts of things the person is and is not capable of doing and (2) determining what should be done to rehabilitate the person.

Research has also been directed at locating the specific deficits of mentally retarded adolescents (A. Brown, Campione, Bray, & Wilcox, 1973; A. Brown, Campione, & Murphy, 1974). The results of these experiments indicate that retardates have difficulty remembering things at least in part because they fail to adopt any kind of efficient rehearsal strategy. When the retardates were *taught* strategies, however, their performance improved. This result is exciting because it suggests that at least in some cases, the deficits of the retardates do not involve the "hardware" of the information-processing system but involve deficits in being able to learn proper strategies—and these are the sorts of deficits that can to some extent be overcome.

Cognitive tasks for evaluating drug effects: Marijuana.   Most drugs affect a person's mental functioning in one way or another. As we know, the mental consequences of most commonly used drugs, such as aspirin or codeine, are relatively minor, amounting perhaps to a slight drowsiness. However, other drugs, such as hallucinogens (LSD, peyote, etc.), affect perception, memory, and thinking in rather dramatic ways.

Psychologists are only beginning to investigate the precise effects of various drugs within the framework of the human information-processing system. In this section, we shall describe some of the research efforts along this line with one particular substance: marijuana. Since the late 1960s there has been a tremendous upsurge in the use of marijuana among middle-class Americans, and therefore the question of "what exactly marijuana does to your mind" is of interest to increasingly large numbers of people. Accordingly, several recent experiments have been designed to explore the effects of marijuana on various aspects of the information-processing system. Two studies (Able, 1971; Darley, Tinklenberg, Roth, Hollister, & Atkinson, 1973b) have been aimed at examining the effects of marijuana on information storage and information retrieval processes. Both experiments arrived at essentially the same conclusions; however, the latter study is somewhat more complete and better controlled; we shall therefore describe it in some detail.

The design of the Darley *et al.* (1973b) study involved two groups of subjects: an experimental group and a control group. Each subject in the experimental group ate a brownie that contained an amount of marijuana calibrated to 20 milligrams of Δ^1-tetrahydrocannabinol, or THC (the "active ingredient" in marijuana). Each subject in the control group ate a placebo brownie that was identical in every respect to the experimental group brownies

Time since drug administration	Experimental procedure
	Presentation and immediate free recall of first ten lists
0 hours	Administration of treatment (Experimental group: marijuana) (Control group: placebo)
1 hour	Delayed free-recall test of first ten lists (both groups)
2 hours	Presentation and immediate free recall of second ten lists (both groups)

FIGURE 8.2   Design for the Darley *et al.* (1973b) experiment.

except that the THC had been removed. There was no way, therefore, for a particular subject to know whether he was in the experimental group or the control group.

The general procedure (depicted in Figure 8.2) involved a series of free-recall tests. Initially, both groups received ten 20-word lists with a free-recall test following each list. Following the ten free-recall tests, either the drug or the placebo was administered to all subjects. An hour later (the point at which the experimental subjects were "most high") a delayed test was administered in which subjects in both groups attempted to recall as many as possible of the 200 words they had seen in the ten initial free-recall lists.

The results of the initial and delayed tests are depicted in Figure 8.3. Because the initial tests occurred prior to administration of the marijuana or placebo, we of course expect no difference between the experimental and control groups in terms of initial free-recall performance—and, in fact, the serial-position curves were identical for the two groups (Figure 8.3a). Of interest, however, is the fact that the two groups did not differ for the *delayed* tests (Figure 8.3b). At the time of the delayed test, subjects in the experimental group were high on marijuana, whereas subjects in the control group were not high on anything. The result shown in Figure 8.3b therefore suggests that marijuana has no effect on retrieval of information already stored in long-term store.[1]

At this point (2 hours after administration of the drug or placebo, while the experimental subjects were still high) subjects in both groups were presented with ten new 20-word lists and received an immediate free-recall test after each list. The results of these tests are shown in Figure 8.3c. There were substantial differences between the two groups: the control (placebo) subjects remembered considerably more than did the experimental (marijuana) subjects. Because from the initial part of the experiment (Figure 8.3b) we have concluded that

[1] A potential flaw in this experiment is that only experienced marijuana users have served as subjects and it can be argued that experienced users have developed strategies for overcoming any retrieval deficits that may accrue under the influence of marijuana. In a strict sense, the conclusions of the study should not be generalized to individuals who are not experienced users of marijuana.

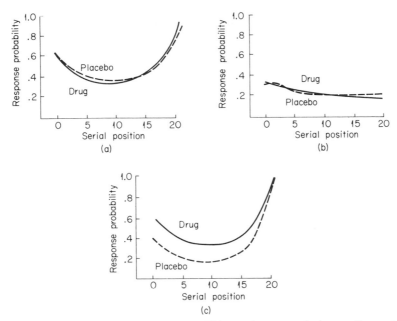

FIGURE 8.3   Results of the Darley *et al.* (1973b) experiment on whether marijuana affects storage or retrieval of information in memory: (a) initial free recall, first ten lists; (b) delayed free-recall, first ten lists; (c) initial free-recall, second ten lists. (After Darley *et al.*, 1973b, Figures 1 and 2.)

marijuana does not affect retrieval processes, the performance differences shown in Figure 8.3c indicate that marijuana must have the effect of reducing the amount of information initially stored in long-term store.

Can we be more precise about the mechanism by which marijuana decreases information storage? A closer look at Figure 8.3c reveals that marijuana does not affect recall from the last two serial positions. Because the last two serial positions are assumed to reflect recall from short-term store (Chapter 3), the implication of this result is that entry of information into short-term store is not impaired by marijuana. Such an implication leads to the conclusion that one consequence of ingesting marijuana is to reduce the transfer of information from short-term store to long-term store. Dovetailing nicely with this conclusion are the results of another experiment (Melges, Tinklenberg, Hollister, & Gillespie, 1970), which indicate that a person's short-term store capacity (digit span) is reduced in direct proportion to the amount of marijuana that the person has taken. To summarize, marijuana appears to impair memory performance by decreasing the amount of information transferred from short-term store to long-term store. The decrease in transfer may be caused at least in part by a reduction in short-term store capacity.

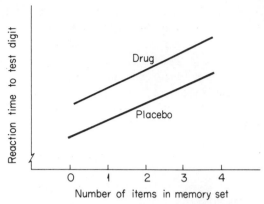

FIGURE 8.4 Results of the Darley *et al.* (1973a) experiment on whether marijuana affects rate of searching through short-term store. (After Darley *et al.*, 1973b, Figures 1 and 2.)

Before we leave the topic of how marijuana affects memory performance, it is worth mentioning one additional experiment performed by Darley, Tinklenberg, Hollister, and Atkinson (1973a).[2] In this study, Darley *et al.* (1973a) have been interested in whether or not marijuana affects the rate of scanning through short-term store. To investigate this question, the Sternberg scanning paradigm (described in Chapter 3) has been used. Remember that in this paradigm, a subject is given a memory set consisting of some variable number of items (for example, digits) following which the subject must make a decision about whether a particular test digit is or is not a member of the memory set. The reaction time to make a decision is then examined as a function of the memory set size.

As in the first Darley *et al.* (1973b) study described above, subjects in an experimental group were given marijuana, whereas subjects in a control group were given a placebo. Figure 8.4 shows the results: the functions relating reaction time to memory set size are shown separately for the marijuana and placebo groups. Both these functions are linear, replicating Sternberg's original findings and implying a sequential search through short-term store. Of interest is the fact that the *slopes* of the reaction time functions are the same for the experimental and the control groups. Because the slope characterizes the search rate through short-term store, this result suggests that search rate is not affected by marijuana. However, the intercept of the marijuana function is raised relative to the intercept of the placebo function, indicating that marijuana must cause an increase in either the time needed to encode the test digit or in the time needed to respond, or both.

---

[2] The reader may wonder why all the marijuana studies seem to be carried out by the same group of people. The reason for this is that the government allows marijuana research to be done by only a small number of researchers whom it deems qualified; and marijuana research can only be done on federal land. The studies described in this chapter have all been run at the Veteran's Administration Hospital in Palo Alto, California.

(In describing the results of this experiment to one of the present authors, Charles Darley remarked that in terms of the functions shown in Figure 8.4, marijuana does not make you steeper—but marijuana does make you higher!)

As we have seen, a simple series of experiments using cognitive tasks can provide a reasonably precise characterization of some of the ways in which marijuana affects the information-processing system. Naturally, there is a good deal more we should like to find out, both about marijuana and about other drugs that enjoy widespread current usage. Unfortunately, however, drug research is a tricky business because of government restrictions and of ethical considerations involving the use of human subjects. In spite of these problems, however, drug research is managing to slowly proceed. It is hoped that at some point in the future, a person who wants to take a drug for medicinal purposes, or for fun, or for insight into the nature of the universe can have a somewhat more scientifically based idea of what he's in for.

EDUCATION

Reasonably precise theories of human memory are useful in education in at least two ways. The first involves the use of computer-assisted instruction (CAI) and, in conjunction with the use of CAI, the creation of programs to optimize the learning process. The second involves the use of paradigms such as semantic memory tasks, to assess how well some particular subject matter has been learned.

Computer-assisted instruction (CAI).   In 1957, Dr. Simon Ramo wrote an article called "A new technique of education," which contained some speculations about the future of education. Picture the high school of the future, said Ramo, in which each student, at registration, receives a specially stamped small plate (like a credit card) that identifies him and his unique course of study. Each day the student would sit down at an "education" machine, insert his card into the machine, and instantly his entire record and progress would be made available to the computer. The machine would then present the next daily lesson to the student.

What would a day be like for such a student? Ramo envisioned students spending some time in rooms with other students and a teacher, but part of their day would be spent with the machine. Progress would be recorded continuously by the machine and a student's program of instruction would be adjusted in accord with his special needs. Furthermore, information from days or weeks of machine operation would form a record that the teacher might use to guide future interaction with the student.

This 1957 article has predicted some of today's CAI systems with a good deal of accuracy. Instead of using a credit card, the student typically types his name and student number on a standard teletype keyboard that is attached to a computer. A computer then presents the student with his lessons, behaving much as a private

FIGURE 8.5   The computer acts like a private tutor in a computer-assisted-instruction system.

tutor does (see Figure 8.5). The computer also keeps records so that a student's progress can be evaluated. Programs such as these are being developed all over the country and are being used in as diverse institutions as prisons and schools for deaf children.

Using computer-assisted instruction to optimize learning.   With CAI as a tool, we can begin to concern ourselves with the question of what the most effective methods are for teaching children new material. In formal terms, this question is one of how learning may be *optimized* and, in general, there are two types of performance that an educator is interested in optimizing. The first is the performance of a given student within a given session and the second is the performance of an entire class during the course. We shall discuss these two types of optimization in turn.

To see what is meant by "optimization within a session" let us suppose that a student is learning German vocabulary words and has a 30-minute session each day to work on the CAI terminal. During a session, the computer presents the vocabulary words to be learned in the form of paired associates. For example, on a given trial, the computer might type out MEAT—?. The student would then attempt to type in the German translation (FLEISCH), and then the computer would type out the entire paired associate (MEAT—FLEISCH). The question of how learning may be optimized now simply boils down to the question of how should the computer choose a word-presentation sequence such that the student learns the maximum possible number of vocabulary words during the session?

A general (and fairly obvious) answer to this question is: at any given time, the computer should concentrate on presenting those words that the student has not yet already learned. That is to say, any presentation of an already learned word is a wasted presentation in the sense that it would have been more efficiently spent presenting an unlearned word. How is the computer to determine which words are and are not already learned? The first thing needed for such a determination is the student's *history* of the correct and incorrect responses on the various words. Without such a history, the computer would be in a hopeless position, for it wouldn't have the slightest inkling of which words have been learned and which have not. However, the computer also needs something else to optimize learning: it needs a mathematically explicit *model* of learning and memory. To get a feel for why this is so, imagine that the computer had only the student's response history. How could it use this history to decide which words have been learned already? One possibility may be to simply assume that any word to which the student has correctly responded in the past must have been learned by the student. However, there are several ways a student can correctly respond to words that he has not really learned. For instance, a word may be responded to only on the basis of information in short-term store. Likewise, the student may have simply guessed and been correct by chance, or the response may have been based on scanty, soon to be forgotten information in long-term store. To distinguish among all these possible "states of learning" the computer must be working within the context of some model that identifies them.

The omnipresent Richard Atkinson has reported an experiment that dramatically illustrates the power of a model of learning and memory used in conjunction with a CAI optimization scheme (Atkinson, 1972a; see also Laubsch, 1970). In Atkinson's experiment, students learned German vocabulary words on a CAI system such as the one described above. The mathematical model used by Atkinson to examine possible optimization strategies corresponds in a rough way to the Atkinson–Shiffrin model (see Atkinson & Crothers, 1964, for a more complete description of the model). The model assumes that at any given time, a particular word is in one of three states: an "unlearned" state, a "transiently learned" state, or a "permanently learned" state. Words in the permanently learned state are responded to (translated) correctly forever. Conversely, words in the unlearned state are translated correctly only by guessing. Finally, words in the transiently learned state are translated correctly, but words in this state had some probability of being forgotten and thereby slipping back into the unlearned state.

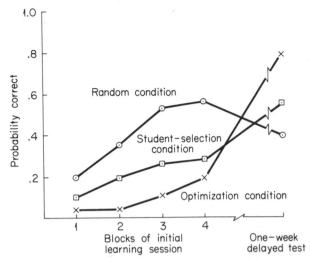

FIGURE 8.6   Results of the Atkinson (1972a) experiment. An optimization scheme in conjunction with a mathematical model of learning and memory produces the best performance. (After Atkinson, 1972a, Figure 1. Copyright 1974 by the American Psychological Association. Reproduced by permission.)

In Atkinson's experiment, the computer's decisions about word-presentation order were determined in four different ways, which corresponded to four different, between-subjects experimental conditions. For the purposes of this discussion, only three of these conditions are of interest. The first two conditions were control conditions, whereas the third was the optimization condition. The three conditions were the following:

Condition 1. The words were simply presented helter skelter in a random order. This control condition is analogous to a vocabulary drill occurring during a typical language class.

Condition 2. The student himself selected which word he wanted presented on any given trial. This condition corresponds to a situation in which a student is given a list of words and told to learn their translations in any way he pleases.

Condition 3. The presentation order was determined by an optimization scheme working in conjunction with the model described above. The optimization scheme arranged presentation order such that, within the context of the model, the maximum possible number of words would be in the permanently learned state by the end of the session.

A week after the learning session, the students were administered a delayed test on all the words that they had been trying to learn. Performance on this delayed test may be viewed as an index of how much was learned and was used as the major criterion for comparing the three presentation conditions.

Figure 8.6 shows the results of Atkinson's experiment. Performance for the three conditions is plotted for the first, second, third, and fourth trial blocks within the experimental session, and at the right is shown the criterion measure of delayed test performance. These results constitute impressive support for the optimization strategy, which has produced by far the most learning as measured by the delayed test. The random condition is the worst and the student-selection condition falls in between.

Why is the order of performance on the delayed test reversed during the learning session itself? The answer to this question is simple. In the optimization condition, the most unlearned (that is, the most difficult) words were continually being selected for presentation and test. Conversely, in the random condition, the words being tested were composed of a mixture of learned and unlearned (easy and difficult) words. Therefore it is no wonder that performance in the random condition was so good relative to performance in the optimization condition. Again, the student-selection condition produced intermediate performance, suggesting that students had the reasonably accurate intuition that they ought to be choosing unlearned, difficult words on which to test themselves. However, the choice dictated by the students' intuitions was not as efficient as the choice dictated by the model.

These results along with numerous others (cf. Atkinson & Paulson, 1972) provides fairly compelling evidence that a model of learning and memory combined with a mathematical optimization strategy can produce substantial increases in learning relative to traditional teaching methods. To illustrate how such a system is incorporated into a larger educational program we shall briefly describe a massive CAI program that is currently being carried out under Atkinson's direction (Atkinson, 1968, 1972b, 1974; Fishman, Keller, & Atkinson, 1968; Atkinson, Fletcher, Lindsay, Campbell, & Barr, 1973).

The project is designed to teach initial reading skills to children in Grades 1–3. A computer, housed at Stanford University, runs CAI terminals in schools near the university and at other schools in Florida, Oklahoma, Texas, and Washington, D.C. Each child spends a 15–30 minute session each day at a CAI terminal. The program consists of a series of eight phrases, with one particular skill being taught during each phase. The skills become progressively more complex, ranging from such very simple ones as identification of single letters (Phase 2), to such fairly complex skills as sentence comprehension (Phase 8). Naturally, each child progresses at his own pace through the program from one phase to the next.

We have already seen how mathematical models can be used to optimize each child's performance within a given session and thereby to get the child through each phase as efficiently and quickly as possible. Now we consider the second question posed at the beginning of this section: suppose a school has only a certain, fixed amount of CAI terminal time available. How should this time be allocated among the various children such that overall class performance is optimized? Let us consider the ingredients needed to answer the question. The first thing needed is some criterion to measure learning performance (analogous to the delayed test in the Atkinson experiment described above). For this purpose, standardized tests have been developed that measure a child's reading ability following the child's participation in a particular phase of the CAI program. Now, using a fairly complex equation, a given child's performance on a standardized test can be predicted as a function of how much total time the child spends on the CAI terminal. This prediction can be made using data gathered from the child's first hour of instruction; therefore in the very initial stage of a class's participation in the CAI program, it is possible to specify how well the class as a whole will eventually do on the standardized test for any given allocation of CAI time among the students. Now the question becomes: what is the educational objective? That is to say, exactly what is it that should be optimized? Although this sounds like a simple question, it's not. Let us consider three possible answers.

1. The most obvious answer seems to be: Allocate time so as to maximize the mean (average) class performance on the standardized test. However, this strategy leads to a problem. For complicated mathematical reasons, optimizing mean class performance is achieved by giving the initially bright children a great deal of instruction at the expense of the initially less bright children. Therefore, this particular objective leads to the socially undesirable consequence of magnifying performance differences among the children.

2. A second possible alternative is to achieve minimum variability across children with respect to reading ability. Unfortunately, however, as may be suspected from the above remarks, this objective can only be achieved by holding back the bright children and concentrating almost exclusively on the less bright children. Mean class performance on the standardized test therefore suffers.

3. The goal that has actually been selected strikes a compromise between Goals 1 and 2. Final class performance on the standardized test is maximized with the restriction that performance variability over children cannot be greater than it would have been with no CAI program at all.

For the purposes of this discussion, however, the major point does not concern precisely which educational goal is chosen, for the question of choosing an educational goal is guided by many considerations—for example, sociological and economic considerations as well as educational considerations. Instead, the point we wish to emphasize is that by using a mathematical optimization strategy, *any* well-defined objective can be achieved. This is probably the major contribution that theory and research in memory and learning can lend to education.

Using semantic memory tasks to assess degree of learning.   As described in Chapter 7, one paradigm used for studying retrieval of information from semantic memory involves presenting a subject with a category (for example, FRUIT) and some restrictor (for example, "first letter, P"). It is then the subject's task to produce an appropriate instance of the category (for example, "pear"). When categories are well learned (as in this example) we expect retrieval of semantic information to consist of two steps. The first step involves going to the location in semantic memory where the relevant category is stored, whereas the second step involves searching within the category to find an appropriate instance. As noted, this retrieval scheme implies that response time to a category–restrictor presentation order (for example, FRUIT–interval–P) should be faster than response time to a restrictor–category presentation order (for example, P–interval–FRUIT), because with the former presentation order the subject is able to execute the first retrieval step (going to the category) during the interval between the presentation of the category name and presentation of the restrictor. This result is invariably found with well-learned categories (Freedman & Loftus, 1971).

What should happen with categories that are not so well learned, for instance, categories that are in the process of being learned? It stands to reason that to the extent that categories are not well learned, the retrieval pattern should bear less resemblance to the retrieval pattern for well-learned categories. In particular, we may expect the advantage of the category–restrictor condition over the restrictor–category condition to decrease, because this advantage is thought to depend on the fact that a subject knows where in memory a particular category is stored. Another way of putting this is that the difference between the two conditions can be used as an index of how well the category has been learned. Such a notion has direct consequences for educational assessment procedures.

An experiment to test this possibility was carried out by the present authors (Loftus & Loftus, 1974a). The subjects in the Loftus–Loftus experiment were graduate students in psychology at the New School for Social Research in New York and the categories used as stimuli were types of psychologists! Specifically, graduate students at the New School learn that a psychologist is associated with one of six different subareas: learning, perception, memory, personality, social, and developmental. The task used involved presentation of one of these areas of psychology and a letter restrictor. The student then, as quickly as possible, had to name a psychologist in the particular area whose name began with the letter. For example, an appropriate response to L–MEMORY or MEMORY–L might be *Loftus* (or *Loess* or *Lockhart*), whereas an appropriate response to P–DEVELOPMENTAL or DEVELOPMENTAL–P might be *Piaget*.

It was expected that as a graduate student learned more about psychology, his semantic memory structure for "psychology" and his retrieval of information from this structure would become more like the structure of and retrieval from well-learned categories such as FRUITS. To explore this possibility, the graduate student subjects were divided into two groups: beginning graduate students and advanced graduate students.

The results of this experiment appear in Figure 8.7 and are very striking. Experienced graduate students exhibited a retrieval pattern that mirrored the usual pattern found for well-learned categories. That is, the category–restrictor condition was faster than the restrictor–category condition. For beginning

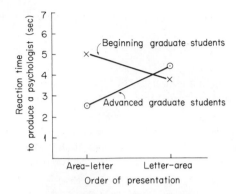

FIGURE 8.7   Results of the Loftus and Loftus (1974a) experiment. Advanced graduate students (O) show a retrieval pattern similar to the retrieval pattern for well-learned categories. Beginning graduate students (×) show the opposite pattern. (After Loftus & Loftus, 1974a, Figure 1. Copyright 1974 by the American Psychological Association. Reproduced by permission.)

graduate students, however, this pattern was actually reversed. The implication is that when a student "learns about" psychology, this learning consists of changing the semantic organization of his knowledge about psychology and/or the process of retrieving information about psychology.

Such a conclusion may be viewed as preliminary and tentative, for the Loftus–Loftus experiment is the only one of its kind. However, the conclusion is interesting in the sense that it suggests a substantial departure from traditional notions about "what is learned" and "what should be tested." In typical educational settings, the student is viewed as learning *facts* and in general, examinations and other devices designed to assess degree of learning test whether or not the student has acquired factual information. It seems reasonable, however, on intuitive, theoretical, and empirical grounds that "what is learned" goes considerably beyond fact acquisition. Indeed, it is the case that the process of learning involves a reorganization of semantic information and implementation of new retrieval schemes. It seems likely that tasks designed within the framework of semantic memory models can measure this broader type of learning, thereby providing a potentially valuable supplement to currently used examination procedures.

HUMAN ENGINEERING

Human engineering is a branch of technology that is concerned with the application of theoretical and experimental psychology to man–machine systems. There are vast numbers of such systems the designs of which can be judiciously directed by the results of psychological inquiry. How, for example, should a typewriter be constructed such that the typist can maximize typing speed and/or minimize errors? How should a computer system be designed so that the computer operator can most easily remember what he is supposed to be doing with all the dials and switches he is staring at? How should the ''Big Board'' at a stock exchange be designed so that an interested stockbroker can read the maximum amount of stock information off the board in the least amount of time?

In the interest of space limitations and for ease of discussion we shall limit our coverage of human engineering to one particular field—that of aviation. We shall see what applications of psychological research have gone into and potentially can go into the design of aviation-related systems.

The pilot's environment.   A large percentage of aviation accidents result from ''human error'' of one sort or another. In Africa, a Boeing 747 crashed because the crew failed to ensure that the leading-edge flaps were extended during takeoff. A Boeing 727 descended through the clouds into Lake Michigan because the pilot misread his altimeter and believed his airplane to be 10,000 feet higher than it actually was. In the worst crash of 1974, another Boeing 727 inbound to Dulles Airport in Washington, D.C. ran into a foggy mountaintop because of a misunderstanding between the pilot and the ground controller who was issuing approach instructions.

These and other unfortunate incidents illustrate a crucial point: a pilot operates in an extremely complex environment that occasionally stretches his memory and information processing capabilities to their limits. The pilot must monitor his instruments, operate controls, and follow complicated instructions from a ground controller—often all at the same time. It is therefore of the utmost importance that the pilot's environment be designed such that it and the pilot's information-processing system can coexist in the most efficient possible manner. We shall briefly discuss past research on how this has been done and we shall speculate about possible future research on how it could be done.

Instrument panels.   A neophyte venturing into an airplane cockpit immediately notices that the instrument panel is immensely complicated. Dials and switches appear to be everywhere. His first question is: how can anyone even learn what all these things are, much less remember them and correctly deal with all the information that they convey? Some reasonably straightforward application of memory and information-processing research suggests design measures that (*a*) allow the configuration of the instrument panel to be learned more easily and (*b*) permit the pilot to efficiently process the information from the instruments during operation.

Aircraft instruments may be conceptually grouped into a hierarchical structure of categories and subcategories, as depicted in Figure 8.8. For example, there are instruments involving aircraft orientation, instruments involving navigation, instruments involving the state of the engines, and so on. Research

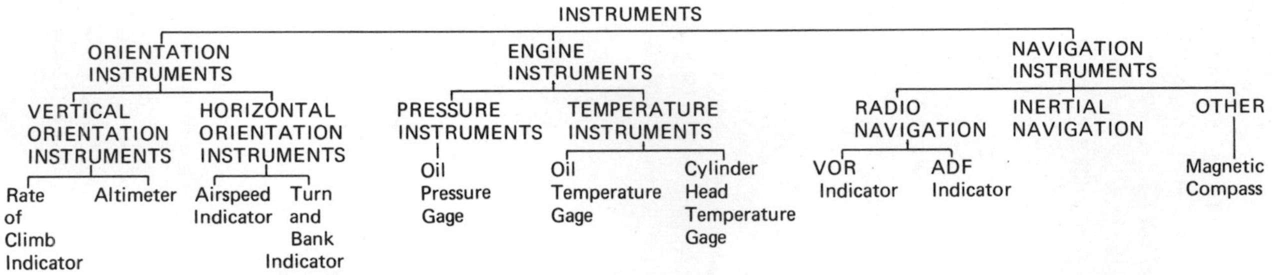

FIGURE 8.8 An example of hierarchical structure in the configuration of aircraft instruments. This is only one possible configuration; there are many others. Also, only a small fraction of the hierarchy is shown.

on category clustering and organization has shown that information corresponding to a large number of items (in this case, aircraft instruments) is both more easily acquired and more resistant to being forgotten if the information is initially organized in some coherent manner (Mandler, 1967; Nelson & Smith, 1972; Tulving, 1968). Therefore, it makes sense to group the instruments according to their inherent hierarchical structure. Navigation instruments go into one cluster and engine instruments go into another cluster. Within the navigation instrument cluster, radio navigation instruments are in one subcluster and inertial navigation instruments are in another subcluster. Within the engine instrument cluster, temperature instruments go into one subcluster and pressure instruments go into another subcluster. And so on. A pilot scanning the panel is then making use of the inherent organization in the information that he is trying to acquire and remember.

Radar screens. A similar argument stemming from research on clustering and organization can be made about the design of the radar screen used by a ground controller. The job of a ground controller is to monitor the positions of many aircraft on his radar screen and issue instructions to the aircraft to prevent them from bumping into one another. How should the controller distribute his attention over the screen? It stands to reason that the amount of attention given to any particular area should depend on the number of aircraft operating within that area. How can the controller most efficiently remember where on his screen there are large concentrations of aircraft? Because this information is changing every few seconds, the problem becomes basically an exercise in maintaining information in short-term store. Research on the topic of short-term store provides suggestions about the design of the screen.

First, the screen should be physically divided up into sections so that the controller can attach a verbal label to each particular area. In practice, screens

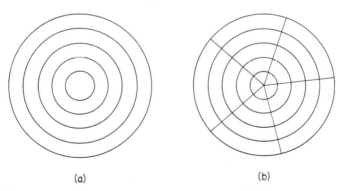

(a)   (b)

FIGURE 8.9 Two possible types of radar screens: (a) a screen divided into five parts; (b) a screen divided into five parts and then subdivided again.

are typically divided up by concentric circles as depicted in Figure 8.9a. How many areas should there be? Research on the memory span (Chapter 3) suggests that seven is about the limit in terms of how many chunks the controller can maintain in short-term store. To be on the safe side, five is probably a better number. However, the fewer the number of areas, the larger each area must be. Therefore, with only five areas, each individual area may not be small enough to permit efficient performance. Again, hierarchical organization can be built in to improve the situation. Suppose that each area is subdivided into smaller subareas using lines drawn radially from the center, as shown in Figure 8.9b. Now the controller can remember how he should be distributing attention over the five major areas—and when working within a specific area, he should be concentrating on some particular subarea.

Pilot–controller communication.   The interchange of information between a pilot and a ground controller bears a formal similarity to the Brown–Peterson short-term memory paradigm (Chapter 3). For example, the controller may suddenly issue the information that the pilot should change his transponder code to 7227 and contact Seattle Approach Control on radio frequency 119.3. The pilot often then has to engage in some kind of distracting activity (for example, scanning the instruments to make sure his airplane is rightside up, listening to additional instructions from the controller, putting down his sandwich, etc.) before responding (carrying out the instructions).[3] It seems likely that research done within the context of the Brown–Peterson paradigm can be applied to improve the pilot's performance in remembering the transmitted information. Currently, such applications are limited and involve for the most part the minimizing of acoustic similarity in the transmitted information (remember from Chapter 3 that acoustically similar information is forgotten more rapidly than acoustically dissimilar information). For example, when numerical information is transmitted, the digit *nine* is transmitted as "niner" in order to distinguish it from the acoustically similar *five*. To transmit alphabetical information, a phonetic alphabet has been developed so, for example, that the acoustically similar BCET is transmitted as the acoustically dissimilar *bravo, charlie, echo, tango*.

Other applications suggest themselves. For example, studies of "release from proactive interference" have shown that when the form of the stimuli to be remembered is changed in some way or another, short-term memory performance improves (Wickens, 1970; see Chapter 3). As the situation stands now, a pilot must remember a series of stimuli composed primarily of digits. In

[3]This similarity was noticed by one of the authors (G. L.) one day when he was flying his Cessna into Seattle–Tacoma Airport. G. L. was issued the instructions described above, at which point he briefly reflected about possible applications of psychological research to pilot–controller communication. After about 15 seconds of reflecting, G. L. discovered that he had forgotten the radio frequency he was supposed to switch to and he had to ask the controller to repeat it.

the example above, the pilot must remember both the transponder code—7227 (transmitted as "seven-two-two-seven")—and also an approach control frequency (transmitted as "one-one-niner-point-three"). There are many ways in which the forms of various types of stimuli could be made more distinguishable from one another. For example, transponder codes could be designated by letters (for example, GBBG) as opposed to digits. Or, transponder codes could always be read in the form of two, two-digit numbers (such as seventy-two, twenty-seven) whereas radio frequencies could still be expressed as a series of single digits.

Another possible improvement might be to designate radio frequencies by letters and to make the letter sequence of a particular frequency correspond systematically to whatever it is that the frequency is used for. For example, the frequency of Seattle Approach Control might be designated by SEAA instead of 119.3. Likewise, the frequency for Seattle-Tacoma control tower might be designated SEAT. Such an innovation would accomplish (at least) three things. First, it would make the form of radio frequency information different from the form of other, numerical information, which should improve short-term memory performance as discussed above. Second, this way of depicting radio frequency information constitutes a recoding scheme that would decrease the number of chunks to be maintained in and recalled from short-term store. In our example, 119.3 constitutes four chunks, whereas SEAA constitutes only two chunks (SEA corresponds to Seattle and A corresponds to Approach Control). Finally, pilots often have to change radio frequencies many times within a short period and a pilot can occasionally forget to whom his radio is tuned. That is, the pilot can look at his radio and see that is tuned to 119.3, but not remember to what 119.3 corresponds. With the scheme described above, however, a glance at the SEAA on the radio makes it immediately apparent that the radio is tuned to Seattle Approach Control.

Theories of short-term memory have not, unfortunately, been specified with a sufficient degree of mathematical precision to allow an a priori evaluation of how effective such innovations as the ones described above would be. However, current theories do suggest the possibility of such innovations, and research is currently being carried out to determine whether their implementation is warranted.

LAW

On April 1, 1909, an interesting trial took place. The plaintiffs were members of the bar of the Supreme Court. The defendant was Hugo Muensterberg, a professor of psychology at the University of Cambridge. The plaintiffs argued that Muensterberg (1908) had published a book entitled *On the Witness Stand* in which untrue and damaging assertions were set forth about the plaintiffs. What exactly had Muensterberg said? A few quotations will give the flavor:

> The lawyer and the judge . . . are sure that they do not need the experimental psychologist. . . . They go on thinking that their instinct and their common sense supplies them with all that is needed and somewhat more. . . . My only purpose is to turn the attention of serious men to an absurdly neglected field [p. 9].

> It seems indeed astonishing that the work of justice is ever carried out in the courts without ever consulting the psychologist and asking him for all the aid which the modern study of suggestion can offer [p. 194].

The plaintiffs argued that this book full of words meant that: (1) psychology had developed very precise methods of determining the accuracy of testimony and of diagnosing guilt. These methods were endorsed by psychologists as applicable to American judicial practice. (2) These methods were superior to those in use in American courts, and by not using these methods lawyers were being grossly negligent.

The plaintiffs argued that Muensterberg's claims were untrue, that their good name had been injured, and they asked for a sum of $1 in compensation for the damage. Their case consisted of providing evidence that (1) the methods of psychology were not very precise, (2) the methods were not generally endorsed as applicable to the American judicial system, (3) the methods had not been shown to be superior to those in use (in fact they were not even available in English-language journals), and (4) the members of the legal profession had not been grossly negligent in rejecting these methods.

The defense attorney argued that his client had not intended any disrespect to the plaintiffs but had wanted to stir them to a sense of their responsibilities.

After the closing arguments, the judge instructed the jury to retire and consult on their verdict. The jurors whispered for an instant, and then announced that they were agreed on a verdict without the need for further deliberation. The foreman then read the verdict: "We find for the plaintiffs, with damages of $1."

Before the courtroom began to clear, the judge expressed his personal view. In no other country in the civilized world, said the judge, had the legal profession taken so little interest in finding out (let alone using) what psychology and other sciences had to offer that might contribute to the American judicial system. That was April 1, 1909.[4]

What can we say now, more than half a century later? Does experimental psychology have something to offer the legal profession? A number of prominent lawyers seem to think so. In one recent textbook on evidence

---

[4]This trial is described in an article written by J. H. Wigmore (1909). It becomes evident that the trial is satirical when the reader learns that the trial took place on April Fool's Day; that the suit has been entered in the Superior Court of Wundt County; and that a Mr. X. Perry Ment has assisted with the defense. Nonetheless, Wigmore's article contains many elements of the legal profession's reaction to Muensterberg's book.

(Louisell, Kaplan, & Waltz, 1972) the chapter on Eyewitness identification contains eight excerpts from the writings of psychologists. A few of the papers deal with recall versus recognition (Postman, Jenkins, & Postman, 1948; Tiernan, 1938). A passage from Bartlett (1932) on how we remember a face is included. An article on identification of the human voice appears too (McGehee, 1937). In his book called *Law and Psychology in Conflict* (1969) lawyer James Marshall has stated that "What is required is social invention in the law based on the findings of the social sciences [p. 117]." Four pages later he argues:

> There is a need for joint research by lawyers and social scientists as to the reliability of evidence which depends upon observation and recollection. Such research should also attempt to answer the question: What possible techniques can be used to avoid the distortions now prevalent in testimony? Effort should be made to reconcile the rules of evidence and conduct of trials with what we know about the nature of perception [p. 121].

Perception and memory of complex events.   What do we know about the nature of memory and perception that may be of interest to an attorney? Consider what happens when a person witnesses a highly complex and sudden event, such as an automobile accident. We already know that his perception, recollection, and verbalization of such an incident is not an identical copy of the original event. We already know that when he recalls a particular event, his memory has gaps, and he continually calls on general knowledge about the world to fill in those gaps (see Chapter 6).

There are numerous ways to influence (and often distort drastically) the recollections of a witness. One relatively easy way is to vary the method by which the recollection is elicited or to vary the form in which questions are asked about the recollection.

Much of the research in this area has indicated that when people are forced to answer specific questions, rather than to report freely, their reports are more complete but less accurate (Cady, 1924; Gardner, 1933; Marquis, Marshall, & Oskamp, 1972; Marston, 1924; Whipple, 1909). Furthermore, the accuracy of an answer to a specific question can be notably influenced by the wording of the question itself. The wording of a question is such an important matter, that a recent book intended to help potential questionnaire designers (Oppenheim, 1966) devotes an entire chapter to the topic of question wording.

In a recent investigation of eyewitness testimony (Loftus & Palmer, 1974), subjects were shown a film of a traffic accident and then they answered questions about the accident. The subjects were interrogated about the speed of the vehicles in one of several ways. For example, some subjects were asked "About how fast were the cars going when they smashed into each other?" whereas others were asked "About how fast were the cars going when they hit each other?" The former question elicited a much higher estimate of speed.

Two interpretations of this finding are possible. First, it is possible that the differential speed estimates result merely from response-bias factors. A subject is uncertain whether to say 10 miles per hour or 20 miles per hour, for example, and the verb "smashed" biases his response toward the higher estimate. A second interpretation is that the question form causes a change in the subject's memory representation of the accident. The verb "smashed" may change the subject's memory such that he actually recalls the accident as being more severe than it has been. If this is the case, we can expect subjects to "remember" other details that have not actually occurred but that are commensurate with an accident occurring at higher speeds.

To distinguish between the two possible interpretations, the subjects were asked to return a week later and, without viewing the film again, they answered a series of questions about the accident. The critical question was "Did you see any broken glass?" There was no broken glass in the accident but, because broken glass would be commensurate with accidents occurring at high speed, we expected that subjects who had been asked the "smashed" question might more often say "Yes" to this critical question. The results (Table 8.2) indicate that those subjects who heard the verb "smashed" were more likely to say "Yes" to the question "Did you see any broken glass?" than were the subjects who heard the verb "hit."

In discussing this finding, Loftus and Palmer have proposed that two kinds of information go into one's memory for some complex occurrence. The first is information gleaned during the perception of the original event; the second is "external" information supplied after the fact. Over time, information from these two sources may be integrated in such a way that we are unable to tell from which source some specific detail is recalled. All we have is one "memory." Discussing the finding in these terms, it appears as though the subject first forms some representation of the accident he has witnessed. The experimenter, then, while asking "About how fast were the cars going when

TABLE 8.2

Distribution of "Yes" and "No" Responses to the
Question "Did you see any broken glass?"[a]

		Verb	
		---	---
		Smashed	Hit
Response	Yes	16	7
	No	34	43

[a] From Loftus and Palmer (1974).

 **"About how fast were the cars going when they SMASHED into each other?"**

FIGURE 8.10 Two types of information in memory: (a) original information; (b) external information; (c) the "memory."

they smashed into each other?'' supplies a piece of "external" information, namely, that the cars have indeed smashed into each other. When these two pieces of information are integrated, a subject has a "memory" of an accident that is more severe than the accident in fact has been, as depicted in Figure 8.10. Because broken glass is typically associated with a severe accident, the subject is more likely to think that broken glass has occurred.

The implication of these results for courtroom examinations, police interrogations, and accident investigations is fairly clearcut. Questions *should* be asked in as neutral a way as possible, to avoid the introduction of "external" information into the witness's memory.

The lineup. In addition to the contribution that information-processing research can make to the legal area of eyewitness testimony, we briefly discuss another issue, which concerns the rights of someone who has been arrested for a crime: the composition of the police lineup.

In the typical lineup procedure, a person who is suspected of having committed a crime is placed among a group of others, and witnesses to the crime are asked to pick out the suspect if they can. The purpose of the lineup is, obviously, to test the witness's ability to recognize the accused person, providing evidence if recognition does occur and exonerating the suspect if it does not. The experience of a witness is similar to that of a subject in a forced-choice recognition memory experiment (Chapter 5). The composition of the lineup is a matter of great importance; how many people are in it, what do the people look like, what are they wearing, all these are crucial issues that can influence the degree to which the lineup is free from suggestive influences and, naturally, determine its value. Whereas the situation is not known to be quite as bad as that depicted in Figure 8.11 it is important that the persons other than the suspect be similar to the suspect in appearance. Otherwise the situation may

FIGURE 8.11   Example of a biased lineup.

be reduced to a recognition test in which the distractors can be immediately rejected as implausible and the suspect is picked by default. (For example, which of the following begins the title of this book: 3, H, +, %?)

SUMMARY

In this chapter, we have touched on some of the ways in which theory and research on human information processing have been applied to real-world problems and we have speculated as to potential future applications. The areas we have discussed have included:

1. *Mental assessment.*   Cognitive tasks may be used to assess the state of a person's mental functioning in various situations. Such tasks may be used to generate a more specific measure of what is now referred to as "intelligence." Additionally, cognitive tasks may be used to pinpoint specific mental deficits arising from such things as retardation, injury, sickness, or ingestion of drugs.

2. *Education.*   Optimization strategies that rest on a mathematical model of memory and learning have been incorporated into computer-assisted instruction systems. Such strategies permit quick and efficient learning, both for an individual child and for a class as a whole. In the field of educational testing, it

has been suggested that semantic memory tasks can be used to assess overall degree of learning in some broadly defined field.

3. *Human engineering*.   Models of memory and information processing may be used to guide the design of man—machine systems. In the field of aviation, the information that must be constantly assimilated and processed by a pilot can be presented in a way that makes optimal use of the inherent organization of the information. Additionally, verbal information that must be transmitted from a ground controller to a pilot can be encoded so as to minimize forgetting on the part of the pilot.

4. *Law*.   Research on reconstruction in memory can be used to design questioning of an individual who has witnessed a complex event. Such questioning procedures, it is hoped, can serve to minimize the degree of distortion that takes place in the witness's memory. Research in the area of recognition memory may be used to guide the makeup of police lineups with the ultimate goal that the witness recognizes a person if and only if the witness has actually seen the person at the time and place of interest.

References

Able, E. L. Marihuana and memory: Acquisition or retrieval? *Science,* 1971, **173,** 1038–040.

Anderson, J. R., & Bower, G. H. Recognition and retrieval processes in free-recall. *Psychological Review,* 1972, **79,** 97–123.

Anderson, J. R., & Bower, G. H. *Human Associative Memory.* Washington, D.C.: V. H. Winston & Sons, 1973.

Anisfeld, M., & Knapp, M. E. Association, synonymity, and directionality in false recognition. *Journal of Experimental Psychology,* 1968, **77,** 171–179.

Atkinson, R. C. Computerized instruction and the learning process. *American Psychologist,* 1968, **23,** 225–239.

Atkinson, R. C. Optimizing the learning of a second-language vocabulary. *Journal of Experimental Psychology,* 1972, **96,** 124–129.   (a)

Atkinson, R. C. Ingredients for a theory of instruction. *American Psychologist,* 1972, **27,** 921–931.   (b)

Atkinson, R. C. Teaching children to read using a computer. *American Psychologist,* 1974, **29,** 169–178.

Atkinson, R. C., & Crothers, E. J. A comparison of paired-associate learning models having different acquisition and retention axioms. *Journal of Mathematical Psychology,* 1964, **2,** 285–315.

Atkinson, R. C., Fletcher, J. D., Lindsay, E. J., Campbell, J. O., & Barr, A. Computer-assisted instruction in initial reading. *Educational Technology,* 1973, **13,** 27–37.

Atkinson, R. C., & Paulson, J. A. An approach to the psychology of instruction. *Psychological Bulletin,* 1972, **78,** 49–61.

Atkinson, R. C., & Shiffrin, R. M. Human memory: A proposed system and its control processes. In K. W. Spence & J. T. Spence (Eds.), *The psychology of learning and motivation: Advances in research and theory.* Vol. 2. New York: Academic Press, 1968.

Atkinson, R. C., & Shiffrin, R. M. The control of short-term memory. *Scientific American,* 1971, **225,** 82–90.

Baddeley, A. The influence of acoustic and semantic similarity in long-term memory for word sequences. *Quarterly Journal of Experimental Psychology,* 1966, **18,** 362–365.

Baddeley, A. D. Effects of acoustic and semantic similarity on short-term paired-associate learning. *Journal of Psychology,* 1970, **61,** 335–343.

Baddeley, A. D., & Warrington, E. K. Amnesia and the distinction between long- and short-term memory. *Journal of Verbal Learning & Verbal Behavior,* 1970, **9,** 176–189.

Banks, W. P. Signal detection theory and human memory. *Psychological Bulletin,* 1970, **74,** 81–99.

Bartlett, F. C. *Remembering: A study in experimental and social psychology*. New York: The Macmillan Co., 1932.

Bernbach, H. A. Decision processes in memory. *Psychological Review*, 1967, **74**, 462–480.

Bjork, E. L., & Healy, A. F. Short-term order and item retention. *Journal of Verbal Learning & Verbal Behavior*, 1974, **13**, 80–97.

Blake, M. Prediction of recognition when recall fails: Exploring the feeling-of-knowing phenomenon. *Journal of Verbal Learning & Verbal Behavior*, 1973, **12**, 311–319.

Bousfield, W. A. The occurrence of clustering in the recall of randomly arranged associates. *Journal of General Psychology*, 1953, **49**, 229–240.

Bousfield, W. A., & Cohen, B. M. The occurrence of clustering in the recall of randomly arranged words of different frequencies of usage. *Journal of Genetic Psychology*, 1955, **52**, 83–95.

Bower, G. H. Organizational factors in memory. *Cognitive Psychology*, 1970, **1**, 18–46.

Bower, G. H. Mental imagery and associative learning. In L. Gregg (Ed.), *Cognition in learning and memory*. New York: John Wiley & Sons, 1973.

Bower, G. H., & Clark, M. C. Narrative stories as mediators for serial learning. *Psychonomic Science*, 1969, **14**, 181–182.

Bower, G. H., & Winzenz, D. Group structure, coding and memory for digit series. *Journal of Experimental Psychology Monograph*, 1969, **80**, No. 2, Part 2, 1–17.

Bransford, J. D., & Franks, J. J. Abstraction of linguistic ideas. *Cognitive Psychology*, 1971, **2**, 331–350.

Briggs, G. Acquisition, extinction and recovery functions in retroactive inhibition. *Journal of Experimental Psychology*, 1954, **47**, 285–293.

Brown, A., Campione, J., Bray, N., & Wilcox, B. Keeping track of changing variables: Effect of rehearsal training and rehearsal prevention in normal and retarded adolescents. *Journal of Experimental Psychology*, 1973, **101**, 123–131.

Brown, A., Campione, J., & Murphy, M. Keeping track of changing variables: Long-term retention of a trained rehearsal strategy by retarded adolescents. *American Journal of Mental Deficiency*, 1974, **78**, 446–453.

Brown, H. B. An experience in identification testimony. *Journal of the American Institute of Criminal Law*, 1935, **25**, 621–622.

Brown, J. Some tests of the decay theory of immediate memory. *Quarterly Journal of Experimental Psychology*, 1958, **10**, 12–21.

Buckhout, R. Psychology and eyewitness identification. Paper presented in a symposium on Psychology and the Law, Western Psychological Association, Portland, Oregon, April 1972.

Buckhout, R. Eyewitness Testimony. *Scientific American*, 1974, **231**, 23–31.

Buschke, H., & Lenon, R. Encoding homophones and synonyms for verbal discrimination and recognition. *Psychonomic Science*, 1969, **14**, 269–270.

Cady, H. M. On the psychology of testimony. *American Journal of Psychology*, 1924, **35**, 110–112.

Cherry, E. C. Some experiments on recognition of speech, with one, and with two ears. *Journal of the Acoustical Society of America*, 1953, **25**, 975–979.

Cofer, C. N., Bruce, D. R., & Reicher, G. M. Clustering in free-recall as a function of certain methodological variations. *Journal of Experimental Psychology*, 1966, **71**, 858–866.

Collins, A. M., & Loftus, E. F. A spreading activation theory of semantic processing. *Psychological Review*, 1975 (in press).

Collins, A. M., & Quillian, M. R. Retrieval time from semantic memory. *Journal of Verbal Learning & Verbal Behavior*, 1969, **8**, 240–247.

Collins, A. M., & Quillian, M. R. Does category size affect categorization time? *Journal of Verbal Learning & Verbal Behavior*, 1970, **9**, 432–436.

Conrad, C. Cognitive economy in semantic memory. *Journal of Experimental Psychology*, 1972, **92**, 149–154.

Conrad, R. Acoustic confusions in immediate memory. *British Journal of Psychology*, 1964, **55**, 75–84.

Conrad, R. Interference or decay over short-term retention intervals? *Journal of Verbal Learning & Verbal Behavior*, 1967, **6**, 49–54.

Conrad, R., & Hull, A. J. Information, acoustic confusion and memory span. *British Journel of Psychology*, 1964, **55**, 429–432.

Craik, F. I. M. The fate of primary memory items in free-recall. *Journal of Verbal Learning & Verbal Behavior*, 1970, **9**, 143–148.

Craik, F. I. M., & Lockhart, R. S. Levels of processing: A framework for memory research. *Journal of Verbal Learning & Verbal Behavior*, 1972, **11**, 671–684.

Craik, F. I. M., & Watkins, M. J. The role of rehearsal in short-term memory. *Journal of Verbal Learning & Verbal Behavior*, 1973, **12**, 598–607.

Darley, C. F., Tinklenberg, J. R., Hollister, L. E., & Atkinson, R. C. Marihuana and retrieval from short-term memory. *Psychopharmacologia*, 1973, **29**, 231–238.   (a)

Darley, C. F., Tinklenberg, J. R., Roth, W. T., Hollister, L. E., & Atkinson, R. C. Influence of marihuana on storage and retrieval processes in memory. *Memory & Cognition*, 1973, **1**, 196–200.   (b)

Darwin, C. J., Turvey, M. T., & Crowder, R. G. An auditory analogue of the Sperling partial-report procedure: Evidence for brief auditory storage. *Cognitive Psychology*, 1972, **3**, 255–267.

Ebbinghaus, H. *Uber das gedächtnis*. Leipzig: Duncker, 1885.

Egan, J. P. *Recognition memory and the operating characteristic*. Technical note AFCRC-TN-58-51. Hearing and Communication Laboratory, Indiana University, 1958.

Egeth, H. Selective attention. *Psychological Bulletin*, 1967, **67**, 41–57.

Elliott, P. B. Tables of d'. In J. A. Swets (Ed.), *Signal Detection and Recognition by Human Observers*. New York: Wiley, 1964.

Estes, W. K. An associative basis for coding and organization in memory. In A. W. Melton & E. Martin (Eds.), *Coding processes in human memory*. Washington, D.C.: Winston, 1972.

Estes, W. K. Phonemic coding and rehearsal in short-term memory for letter strings. *Journal of Verbal Learning & Verbal Behavior*, 1973, **12**, 360–372.

Estes, W. K., & DaPolito, F. J. Independent variation of information storage and retrieval processes in paired-associate learning. *Journal of Experimental Psychology*, 1967, **75**, 18–26.

Fillenbaum, S. Memory for gist: Some relevant variables. *Language & Speech*, 1966, **9**, 217–227.

Fishman, E. J., Keller, L., & Atkinson, R. C. Massed versus distributed practice in computerized spelling drills. *Journal of Educational Psychology*, 1968, **4**, 290–296.

Freedman, J. L., & Loftus, E. F. Retrieval of words from long-term memory. *Journal of Verbal Learning & Verbal Behavior*, 1971, **10**, 107–115.

Freud, S. *Beyond the pleasure principle*. London: International Psychoanalytic Press, 1922.

Freund, R. D., Loftus, G. R., & Atkinson, R. C. Application of multiprocess models for memory to continuous recognition tasks. *Journal of Mathematical Psychology*, 1969, **6**, 576–594.

Gardner, D. S. The perception and memory of witnesses. *Cornell Law Quarterly*, 1933, **8**, 391–409.

Glanzer, M. Storage mechanisms in recall. In G. H. Bower (Ed.), *The psychology of learning and motivation*. New York: Academic Press, 1972.

Glanzer, M., & Cunitz, A. R. Two storage mechanisms in free-recall. *Journal of Verbal Learning & Verbal Behavior*, 1966, **5**, 351–360.

Glanzer, M., & Schwartz, A. Mnemonic structure in free-recall: Differential effects on STS and LTS. *Journal of Verbal Learning & Verbal Behavior*, 1971, **10**, 194–198.

Glass, A. L., & Holyoak, K. J. Alternative conceptions of semantic memory. *Cognition*, 1975 (in press).

Gorman, A. N. Recognition memory for names as a function of abstractness and frequency. *Journal of Experimental Psychology*, 1961, **61**, 23–29.

Green, D. M., & Swets, J. A. *Signal detection theory and psychophysics*. New York: Wiley, 1966.

Grossman, L., & Eagle, M. Synonymity, antonymity, and association in false recognition responses. *Journal of Experimental Psychology*, 1970, **83**, 244–248.

Hall, J. F. Learning as a function of word frequency. *American Journal of Psychology*, 1954, **67**, 138–160.

Hart, J. T. Memory and the memory-monitoring process. *Journal of Verbal Learning & Verbal Behavior*, 1967, **6**, 685–691.

Hayes, J. R. M. Memory span for several vocabularies as a function of vocabulary size. In *Quarterly Progress Report*. Cambridge, Massachusetts: Acoustics Laboratory, Massachusetts Institute of Technology, Jan.–June, 1952.

Hebb, D. O. Distinctive features of learning in the higher animal. In J. Dalafresnaye (Ed.), *Brain mechanisms and learning*. London and New York: Oxford University Press, 1961.

Hellyer, S. Frequency of stimulus presentation and short-term decrement in recall. *Journal of Experimental Psychology*, 1962, **64**, 650.

Hilgard, E. R. Methods and procedure in the study of learning. In S. S. Stevens (Ed.), *Handbook of experimental psychology*. New York: Wiley, 1951.

Hopkins, R. H., & Atkinson, R. C. Priming and the retrieval of names from long-term memory. *Psychonomic Science*, 1968, **11**, 219–220.

Hubel, D. H. & Wiesel, T. N. Receptive fields of single neurons in the cat's striate cortex. *Journal of Physiology*, 1959, **148**, 574–591.

Hubel, D. H., & Wiesel, T. N. Receptive fields, binocular interaction and functional architecture in the cat's visual cortex. *Journal of Physiology*, 1962, **160**, 106–154.

Hunt, E., Frost, N., & Lunneborg, C. Individual differences in cognition: A new approach to intelligence. In G. Bower (Ed.), *The psychology of learning and motivation*. New York: Academic Press, 1973.

Hunt, E., & Lansman, M. Cognitive theory applied to individual differences. In W. K. Estes (Ed.), *Handbook of learning and cognitive processes*. Hillsdale, New Jersey: Lawrence Erlbaum Associates, 1975.

Hunt, E., & Love, T. How good can memory be? In A. W. Melton & E. Martin (Eds.), *Coding processes in human memory*. Washington, D.C.: Winston, 1972.

Hunt, E., Lunneborg, C., & Lewis, J. What does it mean to be high-verbal? *Cognitive Psychology*, 1975 (in press).

James, W. *The principles of psychology*. New York: Henry Holt & Co., 1890.

Jenkins, J. G., & Dallenbach, K. M. Obliviscence during sleep and waking. *American Journal of Psychology*, 1924, **35**, 605–612.

Katz, J. J., & Fodor, J. A. The structure of semantic theory. *Language*, 1963, **39**, 170–210.

Keppel, G., & Underwood, B. J. Proactive inhibition in short-term retention of single items. *Journal of Verbal Learning & Verbal Behavior*, 1962, **1**, 153–161.

King, D. L., & Pontious, R. H. Time relations in the recall of events of the day. *Psychonomic Science*, 1969, **17**, 339–340.

Kinsbourne, M., & George J. The mechanism of the word-frequency effect on recognition memory. *Journal of Experimental Psychology*, 1968, **78**, 481–487.

Kinsbourne, M., & George, J. The mechanism of the word-frequency effect on recognition memory. *Journal of Verbal Learning & Learning Behavior*, 1974, **13**, 63–69.

Kintsch, W. An experimental analysis of single stimulus tests and multiple-choice tests of recognition memory. *Journal of Experimental Psychology*, 1968, **76**, 1–6.

Kintsch, W. *Learning, memory and conceptual processes*. New York: Wiley, 1970.   (a)

Kintsch, W. Models for free recall and recognition. In D. A. Norman (Ed.), *Models of human memory*. New York: Academic Press, 1970. (b)

Kintsch, W. Notes on the structure of semantic memory. In E. Tulving & W. Donaldson (Eds.), *Organization of memory*. New York: Academic Press, 1972.

Kintsch, W. *The representation of meaning in memory*. Hillsdale, New Jersey: Lawrence Erlbaum Associates, 1974.

Kintsch, W., & Buschke, H. Homophones and synonyms in short-term memory. *Journal of Experimental Psychology*, 1969, **80**, 403–407.

Lakoff, G. Hedges: A study in meaning criteria and the logic of fuzzy concepts. Papers from the Eighth Regional Meeting, Chicago Linguistic Society. Chicago: University of Chicago Linguistic Department, 1972.

Laubsch, J. A. Optimal item allocation, in computer-assisted instruction. *IAG Journal*, 1970, **3**, 295–311.

Laurence, M. W. Role of homophones in transfer learning. *Journal of Experimental Psychology*, 1970, **86**, 1–7.

Lindsay, P. H., & Norman, D. A. *Human information processing: An introduction to psychology*. New York: Academic Press, 1972.

Lockhart, R. S., & Murdock, B. B. Jr. Memory and the theory of signal detection. *Psychological Bulletin*, 1970, **74**, 100–109.

Loftus, E. F. Activation of semantic memory. *American Journal of Psychology*, 1973, **86**, 331–337. (a)

Loftus, E. F. How to catch a zebra in semantic memory. Paper presented at the Minnesota Conference on Cognition, Knowledge, and Adaptation. Minneapolis, Minn., 1973. (b)

Loftus, E. F. Reconstructing memory: The incredible eyewitness. *Psychology Today*, 1974, **8**, 116–119.

Loftus, E. F., & Loftus, G. R. Changes in memory structure and retrieval over the course of instruction. *Journal of Educational Psychology*, 1974, **66**, 315–318. (a)

Loftus, E. F., & Palmer, J. C. Reconstruction of automobile destruction: An example of the interaction between language and memory. *Journal of Verbal Learning & Verbal Behavior*, 1974, **13**, 585–589.

Loftus, E. F., & Zanni, G. Eyewitness testimony: The influence of the wording of a question. *Bulletin of the Psychonomic Society*, 1975, **5**, 86–88.

Loftus, G. R. Comparison of recognition and recall in a continuous memory task. *Journal of Experimental Psychology*, 1971, **91**, 220–226.

Loftus, G. R., & Loftus, E. F. The influence of one memory retrieval on a subsequent memory retrieval. *Memory & Cognition*, 1974, **3**, 467–471. (b)

Loftus, G. R., & Patterson, K. K. Components of short-term proactive interference. *Journal of Verbal Learning & Verbal Behavior*, 1975, **14**, 105–121.

Louisell, D. W., Kaplan, J., & Waltz, J. R. *Cases and materials on evidence*. (2nd ed.) Mineola, New York: The Foundation Press, 1972.

MacDougall, R. Recognition and recall. *Journal of Philosophy*, 1904, **1**, 299–333.

Mandler, G. Organization and memory. In K. W. Spence & J. T. Spence (Eds.), *The psychology of learning and motivation: Advances in research and theory*, Vol. 1. New York: Academic Press, 1967.

Marquis, K., Marshall, J., & Oskamp, S. Testimony validity as a function of question form, atmosphere and item difficulty. *Journal of Applied Social Psychology*, 1972, **2**, 167–186.

Marshall, J. *Law and psychology in conflict*. New York: Anchor Books, 1969.

Marston, W. W. Studies in testimony. *Journal of Criminal Law & Criminology*, 1924, **15**, 5–31.

McDougall, W. The sensations excited by a single momentary stimulation of the eye. *British Journal of Psychology*, 1904, **1**, 78–113.

McGehee, F. The reliability of the identification of the human voice. *Journal of General Psychology*, 1937, **17**, 249–271.

McWhirter, N., & McWhirter, R. *Guinness book of world records*. New York: Bantam, 1973.

Melges, F. T., Tinklenberg, J. R., Hollister, L. E. & Gillespie, H. K. Marihuana and temporal disintegration. *Science*, 1970, **168**, 1118–1120.

Meyer, D. E. On the representation and retrieval of stored semantic information. *Cognitive Psychology*, 1970, **21**, 242–300.

Miller, G. A. The magical number seven, plus or minus two: Some limits on our capacity to process information. *Psychological Review*, 1956, **63**, 81–97.

Milner, B. R. Amnesia following operation on temporal lobes. In C. W. N. Whitty and O. L. Zurgwill (Eds.) *Amnesia*. London: Butterworths, 1966.

Moray, N. Attention in dichotic listening: Affective cues and the influence of instructions. *Quarterly Journal of Experimental Psychology*, 1959, **11**, 59–60.

Moray, N., Bates, A., & Barnett, I. Experiments on the four-eared man. *Journal of the Acoustical Society of America*, 1965, **38**, 196–201.

Morgan, C. S. A study in the psychology of testimony. *Journal of the American Institute of Criminal Law*, 1917, **8**, 222.

Muensterburg, H. *On the witness stand*. New York: McClure, 1908.

Murdock, B. B. Jr. The serial position effect in free-recall. *Journal of Experimental Psychology*, 1962, **64**, 482–488.

Neisser, U. Decision-time without reaction-time. *American Journal of Psychology*, 1963, **76**, 376–385.

Neisser, U. Visual search. *Scientific American*, 1964, **210**, 94–102.

Neisser, U. *Cognitive psychology*. New York: Appleton-Century-Crofts, 1967.

Neisser, U., Novick, R., & Lazar, R. Searching for ten targets simultaneously. *Perceptual & Motor Skills*, 1963, **17**, 955–961.

Nelson, T. O., & Rothbart, R. Acoustic savings for items forgotten from long-term memory. *Journal of Experimental Psychology*, 1972, **93**, 357–360.

Nelson, T. O., & Smith, E. E. Acquisition and forgetting of hierarchically organized information in long-term memory. *Journal of Experimental Psychology*, 1972, **95**, 288–396.

Norman, D. A. Toward a theory of memory and attention. *Psychological Review*, 1968, **75**, 522–536.

Norman, D. A. "Remembrance of things past." Technical report 11, Department of Psychology, University of California, San Diego, 1970.

Oppenheim, A. N. *Questionnaire design and attitude measurement*. New York: Basic Books, 1966.

Parks, T. E. Signal detectability theory and recognition memory performance. *Psychological Review*, 1966, **73**, 44–58.

Pavlov, I. *Conditioned Reflexes*. London and New York: Oxford University Press, 1927.

People vs. Capon. Supreme Court of Illinois, 1961. 23 Ill. 2d 254,178 N.E. 2d 296.

Peterson, L. R., & Peterson, M. J. Short-term retention of individual verbal items. *Journal of Experimental Psychology*, 1959, **58**, 193–198.

Pollack, I. The assimilation of sequentially coded information. *American Journal of Psychology*, 1953, **66**, 421–435.

Posner, M. I. Short-term memory systems in human information processing. *Acta Psychologica (Amsterdam)*, 1967, **27**, 267–284.

Postman, L. Choice behavior and the process of recognition. *American Journal of Psychology*, 1950, **63**, 443–447.

Postman, L. One-trial learning. In C. N. Cofer & B. S. Musgrave (Eds.), *Verbal behavior and learning*. New York: McGraw-Hill, 1963.

Postman, L., Adams, P. A., & Phillips, L. W. Studies in incidental learning II. The effects of association value and method of testing. *Journal of Experimental Psychology*, 1955, **49**, 1–10.

Postman, L., Jenkins, W. O., & Postman, D. L. An experimental comparison of active recall and recognition. *American Journal of Psychology*, 1948, **61**, 511.

Postman, L., & Phillips, L. W. Short-term temporal changes in free-recall. *Quarterly Journal of*

Experimental Psychology, 1965, **17**, 132–138.

Postman, L., & Underwood, B. J. Critical issues in interference theory. *Memory & Cognition*, 1973, **1**, 19–40.

Puff, C. R. Clustering as a function of sequential organization of stimulus word lists. *Journal of Verbal Learning & Verbal Behavior*, 1966, **5**, 503–506.

Ramo, S. A new technique of education. *Engineering & Science Monthly*, 1957, **21**, 17–22.

Rips, L. J., Shoben, E. J., & Smith, E. E. Semantic distance and the verification of semantic relations. *Journal of Verbal Learning & Verbal Behavior*, 1973, **12**, 1–20.

Rosch, E. On the internal structure of perceptual and semantic categories. In T. E. Moore (Ed.), *Cognitive development and acquisition of language*. New York: Academic Press, 1973.

Rumelhart, D. E., Lindsay, P. H., & Norman, D. A. A process model for long-term memory. In E. Tulving & W. Donaldson (Eds.), *Organization of memory*. New York: Academic Press, 1972.

Rundus, D. Analysis of rehearsal processes in free-recall. *Journal of Experimental Psychology*, 1971, **89**, 63–77.

Rundus, D., & Atkinson, R. C. Rehearsal processes in free-recall: A procedure for direct observation. *Journal of Verbal Learning & Verbal Behavior*, 1970, **9**, 99–105.

Rundus, D., Loftus, G. R., & Atkinson, R. C. Immediate free-recall and three-week delayed recognition. *Journal of Verbal Learning & Verbal Behavior*, 1970, **9**, 684.

Sachs, J. Recognition memory for syntactic and semantic aspects of connected discourse. *Perception & Psychophysics*, 1967, **2**, 437–442.

Shannon, C. E., & Weaver, W. *The mathematical theory of communication*. Urbana, Ill.: University of Illinois Press, 1949.

Shepard, R. N. Recognition memory for words, sentences and pictures. *Journal of Verbal Learning & Verbal Behavior*, 1967, **6**, 156–163.

Shiffrin, R. M. Forgetting: Trace erosion or retrieval failure? *Science*, 1970, **168**, 1601–1603.   (a)

Shiffrin, R. M. Memory Search. In D. A. Norman (Ed.), *Models of human memory*. New York: Academic Press, 1970.   (b)

Smith, E. E., Barresi, J., & Gross, A. C. Imaginal versus verbal coding and the primary-secondary memory distinction. *Journal of Verbal Learning & Verbal Behavior*, 1971, **10**, 597–603.

Smith, E. E., Shoben, E. J., & Rips, L. J. Structure and process in semantic memory: A featural model for semantic decisions. *Psychological Review*, 1974, **81**, 214–241.

Sperling, G. The information available in brief visual presentations. *Psychological Monographs*, 1960, **74**, 1–29.

Sperling, G. A model for visual memory tasks. *Human Factors*, 1963, **5**, 19–39.

Sperling, G. Successive approximations to a model for short-term memory. *Acta Psychologica*, 1967, **27**, 285–292.

Sperling, G., Budiansky, J., Spivak, J., & Johnson, M. C. The maximum rate of scanning letters for the presence of a numeral. *Science*, 1971, **174**, 307–311.

Sperling, G., & Speelman, R. G. Acoustic similarity and auditory short-term memory: Experiments and a model. In D. A. Norman (Ed.), *Models of human memory*. New York: Academic Press, 1970.

Sternberg, S. High-speed scanning in human memory. *Science*, 1966, **153**, 652–654.

Sternberg, S. Two operations in character-recognition: Some evidence from reaction-time measurements. *Perception & Psychophysics*, 1967, **2**, 45–53.

Sternberg, S. Mental processes revealed by reaction-time experiments. *American Scientist*, 1969, **57**, 421–457.   (a)

Sternberg, S. The discovery of processing stages. Extensions of Donder's method. *Acta Psychologica*, 1969, **30**, 276–315.   (b)

Sumby, W. H. Word frequency and serial position effects. *Journal of Verbal Learning & Verbal Behavior*, 1963, **1**, 443–450.

Swets, J. A. (Ed.) *Signal detection and recognition by human observers: Contemporary readings*. New York: Wiley, 1964.

Swets, J. A., Tanner, W. P. Jr., & Birdsall, T. G. Decision processes in perception. *Psychological Review*, 1961, **68**, 301–340.

Tieman, D. G. "Recognition memory for comparative sentences." Unpublished doctoral dissertation, Stanford University, 1971.

Tiernan, J. J. The principle of closure in terms of recall and recognition. *American Journal of Psychology*, 1938, **51**, 97–108.

Tomkins, S. S. A theory of memory. In J. S. Antrobus (Ed.), *Cognition and affect*. Boston: Little, Brown & Co., 1970.

Tulving, E. Subjective organization in free-recall of "unrelated" words. *Psychological Review*, 1962, **69**, 344–354.

Tulving, E. Theoretical issues in free-recall. In T. Dixon & D. Horton (Eds.), *Verbal behavior and general behavior theory*. Englewood Cliffs, New Jersey: Prentice-Hall, 1968.

Tulving, E. Episodic and semantic memory. In E. Tulving & W. Donaldson (Eds.), *Organization of memory*. New York: Academic Press, 1972.

Tulving, E., & Pearlstone, Z. Availability versus accessibility of information in memory for words. *Journal of Verbal Learning & Verbal Behavior*, 1966, **5**, 381–391.

Tulving, E., & Thomson, D. M. Retrieval processes in recognition memory; Effect of associative context. *Journal of Experimental Psychology*, 1971, **87**, 116–124.

Tulving, E., & Thomson, D. M. Encoding specificity and retrieval processes in episodic memory. *Psychological Review*, 1973, **80**, 352–373.

Tversky, B. Encoding processes in recognition and recall. *Cognitive Psychology*, 1973, **5**, 275–287.

Underwood, B. J. Retroactive and proactive inhibition after five and fourty-eight hours. *Journal of Experimental Psychology*, 1948, **38**, 29–38. (a)

Underwood, B. J. "Spontaneous recovery" of verbal associations. *Journal of Experimental Psychology*, 1948, **38**, 429–439. (b)

Underwood, B. J. Proactive inhibition as a function of time and degree of prior learning. *Journal of Experimental Psychology*, 1949, **39**, 24–34.

Underwood, B. J. Forgetting. *Scientific American*, reprint 482. 1964.

Underwood, B. J. False recognition produced by implicit verbal responses. *Journal of Experimental Psychology*, 1965, **70**, 122–129.

Wanner, H. E. "On remembering, forgetting, and understanding sentences." Unpublished doctoral dissertation, Harvard University, 1968.

Watkins, M. J., & Watkins, O. C. Processing of recency items for free-recall. *Journal of Experimental Psychology*, 1974, **102**, 488–493.

Waugh, N. C., & Norman, D. A. Primary memory. *Psychological Review*, 1965, **72**, 89–97.

Whipple, G. M. The observer as reporter: A survey of the psychology of testimony. *Psychological Bulletin*, 1909, **6**, 153–170.

Whipple, G. M. *Manual of physical and mental tests. Volume I—Simpler processes*. Baltimore: Warwick and York, 1914.

Wickens, D. D. Encoding categories of words: An emprical approach to meaning. *Psychological Review*, 1970, **77**, 1–15.

Wickens, D. D. Characteristics of word encoding. In A. W. Melton & E. Martin (Eds.), *Coding processes in human memory*. Washington, D.C.: Winston, 1972.

Wickens, D. D., Born, D. G., & Allen, C. K. Proactive inhibition and item similarity in short-term memory. *Journal of Verbal Learning & Verbal Behavior*, 1963, **2**, 440–445.

Wickens, D. D., Ory, N. E., & Graf, S. A. Encoding by taxonomic and acoustic categories in long-term memory. *Journal of Experimental Psychology*, 1970, **84**, 462–469.

Wickelgren, W. A. Acoustic similarity and intrusion errors in short-term memory. *Journal of Experimental Psychology*, 1965, **70**, 102–108.

Wigmore, J. H. Professor Muensterberg and the psychology of testimony. *Illinois Law Review*, 1909, **3**, 399–445.

Wilkins, A. J. Conjoint frequency, category size, and categorization time. *Journal of Verbal*

Learning & Verbal Behavior, 1971, **10,** 382–385.

Woodward, A. E., Bjork, R. A., & Jongeward, R. H. Recall and recognition as a function of primary rehearsal. *Journal of Verbal Learning & Verbal Behavior*, 1973, **12,** 608–617.

Yaroush, R., Sullivan, M. J., & Ekstrand, B. R. Effect of sleep on memory. II: Differential effect of the first and second half of the night. *Journal of Experimental Psychology*, 1971, **88,** 361–366.

Zeller, A. F. An experimental analogue of repression: The effect of individual failure and success on memory measured by relearning. *Journal of Experimental Psychology,* 1950, **40,** 411–422.

Author Index

The numbers in *italics* refer to the pages on which the complete reference is listed.

173

Subject Index

A
Aviation, 153–157

B
Binary digits, 44
Bits, 3, 43–44

C
Chunk, 44–48, 55, 69, 156
Classical conditioning, 77
Cocktail party phenomenon, 31
Cognitive economy, 125, 128
Computer-assisted instruction (CAI), 145–150
Computers, 5–6
    computer analogy of short-term memory, 47
    hardware vs. software, 6
    programs, 6
Conditioned response, 77
Conditioned stimulus, 77
Connected discourse, 108
Consonant trigram, 39

D
Dichotic listening experiments, 31
Drug effects, 141–145

E
Echoic store, 11, 19–21, 32, 48
Education, 145, 162
Episodic memory, 119, 134–135

E
Extinction, 77
Eyewitness testimony, 116–117, 159–163

F
Feature-comparison model, 130–134
Feature-detection analysis, 23
Features, defining vs. characteristic, 130
Feeling of knowing, 89
Fixations, eye, 12
Free recall, 35
    multitrial, 68
    organization in, 66
    in Rundus experiments, 58

G
GL loves BF, 2
Guinness' Book of Records, 1

H
Human engineering, 152–157, 163

I
Iconic store, 11 ff., 21, 28, 48, 50
Individual differences, 137–140
Information, 1, 3–4, 43–44
    visual vs. auditory vs. tactile vs. olfactory vs. gustatory, 11
Information processing, 3
Information Theory, 3

177